PENGUIN PASSNOTES

Animal Farm

Dr Stephen Coote was educated at Magdalene College, Cambridge, where he was an exhibitioner, and at Birkbeck College, University of London, where he was the senior research scholar. He was principal of tutorial colleges in both London and Oxford, and an examiner. He is currently Advisory Editor of Penguin Passnotes. Dr Coote has written a number of guides to Shakespeare's plays in this series, as well as to the works of Chaucer and Emily Brontë.

PENGUIN PASSNOTES

GEORGE ORWELL

Animal Farm

S. H. COOTE M.A., PH.D.

PENGUIN BOOKS

PENGUIN BOOKS

Published by the Penguin Group
27 Wrights Lane, London W8 5TZ, England
Viking Penguin Inc., 40 West 23rd Street, New York, New York 10010, USA
Penguin Books Australia Ltd, Ringwood, Victoria, Australia
Penguin Books Canada Ltd, 2801 John Street, Markham, Ontario, Canada L3R 1B4
Penguin Books (NZ) Ltd, 182–190 Wairau Road, Auckland 10, New Zealand

Penguin Books Ltd, Registered Offices: Harmondsworth, Middlesex, England

First published 1990

Made and printed in Great Britain by
Richard Clay Ltd, Bungay, Suffolk

Filmset in Monophoto Erhardt

for Alexander and Phoebe

Contents

To the Student

This book is designed to help you with your GCSE English Literature examination. It contains an introduction to the life and thoughts of George Orwell as well as to the background of *Animal Farm* itself. It also offers a chapter-by-chapter analysis and a commentary on the characters and the main themes.

When you use this book remember that it is no more than an aid to your study. It will help you to find passages quickly and perhaps give you some ideas for essays and project work. But remember: *this book is not a substitute for reading the novel, and it is your response and your knowledge that matter.* These are the things that the examiners are looking for, and they are also the things that will give you the most pleasure. Show your knowledge and appreciation to the examiners, and show them clearly.

Introduction: *George Orwell and the background to* Animal Farm

THE MAKING OF GEORGE ORWELL

Orwell's real name was Eric Blair. He was born in 1903, and for his first twenty-four years he lived the seemingly conventional existence of a young man from the English middle classes. He was sent to preparatory school, to Wellington, and then to Eton. In these places he was educated for his role as a future civil servant, one of the men who would help govern Britain's vast overseas empire. His father had worked in the Civil Service in India, and it seemed only natural that his son should follow suit. In 1922 young Blair went out to Burma as a member of the Indian Imperial Police.

He loathed what he saw. He loathed the idea that the British should rule vast areas of the world that did not belong to them and that they also exploited them for the profits they could make. He loathed the injustice and poverty this entailed. He loathed the people who permitted these to continue, describing them on one occasion as 'dull, boozing, witless porkers'. The association between pigs and capitalists – capitalists are people who own large amounts of capital, with which they run factories, farms and other industries – became fixed in his mind. It achieved its supreme expression in *Animal Farm*.

Eventually Blair resigned from the Indian Police and returned to England, vowing he would become a writer. He had always known that this was his true vocation. He now realized that he must begin.

What would he write about? Blair had seen exploitation in Burma. Now he wanted to get to know its equivalent in England. He set out to see aspects of life in his own country that most people of his background were protected from. He went to live among the tramps. Later he went to Paris. Here he ran out of money and took a job washing-up in an expensive hotel. He eventually recorded these experiences in an important book: *Down and Out in Paris and London* (1933). Blair had hugely expanded his horizons. In effect he had made himself a new man. He felt he needed a new name to symbolize this change. 'I rather favour George Orwell' he wrote.

Orwell was to develop a deepening sympathy for the ordinary working people of his country and their sufferings. In the 1930s these were particularly acute. The country was in deep financial trouble. There was widespread poverty and unemployment. In *The Road to Wigan Pier* (1937) Orwell offers a sharply critical and detailed account of these.

While he was writing *The Road to Wigan Pier*, Orwell came into direct contact with the political ideas that motivated many of the working people in his country. Basically there were two extreme views. Many people looked to Russia for their lead, seeing in the communist system and its ideals the only hope for a fairer future. Others looked to the fascists and to Hitler's Germany. In England this way of thought was popularized by Oswald Mosley. It was when Orwell heard Mosley speaking – and he was a powerful orator – that he realized how easily people could be duped by a few carefully chosen political lies. This made a deep impression on Orwell and has an important part to play in *Animal Farm*.

It was at this time that Orwell married and bought his own farm, which he worked while continuing with his writing. He kept various animals – including a goat called Muriel – but it was the pigs, once again, that most stirred his imagination. He described their greed with fascinated revulsion and was glad when the time came to send them off to the butcher.

Orwell did not spend long on his farm. A civil war had broken out in Spain between the fascist supporters of Franco and the various groups of left-wing fighters who supported the cause of the ordinary working people. Like many of the intellectuals of the time Orwell realized he must go and see at first hand what was happening. He joined the Workers' Party for Marxist Unity, fighting in support of the Republicans, and was soon wounded. When he recovered, he learned that many of his comrades had been betrayed by their own side and shot.

Orwell was deeply shocked. Any sympathy he might have had with Soviet communism evaporated in the heat of his hatred. The Soviets had quite simply abandoned their supporters in Spain because they had realized that it was not to their advantage to encourage a communist revolution there. In other words, the politics of the Soviet communists were entirely dictated by the pursuit of personal power and convenience.

In his fury and disillusion Orwell wrote another important book: *Homage to Catalonia* (1938). The book was not a success, though it is now recognized as a classic. Quite simply, many British people (especially those of a left-wing persuasion) did not want to hear criticism of their much-admired Russia.

Orwell was convinced that it was a writer's duty to tell people uncomfortable truths. He was certain that if people of a left-wing persuasion looked to communist Russia as a guide, they would be deceived. Russia was not an ideal communist state; she was a tyranny. The ideals of the revolution had been betrayed by the monstrous cruelties of Joseph Stalin. But few people would believe this, especially during the Second World War, when the Russians fought with immense bravery against the forces of Hitler and so prevented him from focusing all his attention on the invasion of England. The Russians were regarded as heroes. The newspapers were carefully censored to make sure that only glowing reports of Russian life reached the British people. Orwell became more than ever convinced that it was his duty to tell the truth.

He wrote: 'The business of making people *conscious* of what is happening outside their own small circle is one of the major problems of our time; a new literary technique will have to be evolved to meet it.' That search for a new technique eventually resulted in the writing of *Animal Farm*.

This short novel is what is sometimes called a 'satiric beast fable'. Like such great writers of the past as Aesop, Chaucer and La Fontaine, Orwell portrays a world in which animals represent human characteristics. This allows these characteristics to be presented sharply and clearly. By showing us a world of animals and the corruption of their high ideals, Orwell can show us how the world of human ideals is also betrayed, with the result that man inflicts terrible suffering on his own kind.

In *Animal Farm* the pigs represent the forces of communism. In particular Napoleon represents the evil genius of Stalin, who corrupted the Russians' dream of freedom into a nightmare. Since the background of Russian communism is so important to Orwell's novel, it will be useful if we here give a short account of what actually happened in Russia. This will then help us to understand the events that Orwell is exposing and satirizing in his novel.

THE RUSSIAN REVOLUTION AND *ANIMAL FARM*

Ideas are the most powerful of human creations. It is with ideas that we change the world. Of all the ideas that have changed the modern world, communism is among the most influential.

The ideas of communism were developed from the notions of Karl Marx. Marx was a nineteenth-century thinker. He considered himself to be a scientist and believed he had discovered the unchanging laws of human progress. Today scientists no longer believe in 'unchanging laws', and so we can no longer think of Marx as a true scientist. He none the less remains a man of huge intelligence and insight and one of the great shaping forces of the twentieth century.

We have seen that Marx believed in progress, the idea that human life must change and that those changes can be accurately plotted. Whether people want them or not, the changes will come about. There is no choice in the matter. Marx did not believe that people really have freedom of choice. That is partly why his ideas are so loathed by the democratic countries of western Europe. Democracies are based on freedom of choice. In particular they are based on elections. When you are eighteen, you will be able to vote; you will be able to say whether you approve of the government in power or whether you want to change it. One of the first things Napoleon does when he comes to power in *Animal Farm* is to abolish free elections. For him, democracy is a waste of time.

Marx believed that he and his contemporaries were living in the 'age of capitalism'. This was the period when a small miniority of people owned all the money or 'capital' that was needed to make goods and sell them. Marx was keenly aware of the injustices of this system, particularly when nobody tried to control it. He was especially horrified that the ordinary working people whom the capitalists employed should be so poor, so hard-worked and so little able to share in the wealth they had created. He argued that one day the great mass of these ordinary people – the proletariat – would rise up and abolish their capitalist masters for ever. This is the inevitable change he foresaw, and this is exactly what old Major (Orwell's representation of Marx in his novel) suggests the animals should bring about. You may like to compare Major's speech in Chapter One to this passage from the Communist Manifesto, which tells how communists must:

openly declare that their ends can be attained only by the forcible overthrow of all existing social conditions. Let the ruling classes tremble at the Communistic revolution. The proletarians have nothing to lose but their chains. They have a world to win. WORKING MEN OF ALL COUNTRIES, UNITE!

A revolution of this sort had been brewing in Russia ever since the middle of the nineteenth century. In 1917, as the horrors of the First World War were coming to their end, it seemed ready to erupt. Eventually, under the leadership of Lenin, the Russian communists or Bolsheviks seized power from the Tsar and set up a dictatorship of the proletariat. The way to a new and free world for the ordinary people seemed clear, just as it does in *Animal Farm* when the beasts have expelled Mr Jones. The 'age of capitalism' has been replaced by the 'age of socialism'. Progress has worked its change. Heaven on earth will soon come about.

Or will it? It soon became clear that the 'dictatorship of the proletariat' in Russia really meant the dictatorship of the Bolshevik party. Similarly, in *Animal Farm*, rule by the animals themselves really means rule by the pigs. And, just as the death of Lenin resulted in a power struggle in Russia between the two leading Bolsheviks, Stalin and Trotsky, so in *Animal Farm* there is a power struggle between the two leading pigs, Napoleon and Snowball. These two pigs pay lip service to the idea that 'all animals are equal'. What they are really seeking is personal power. Orwell viewed Trotsky and Stalin in exactly the same way.

Stalin and Trotsky disagreed over several fundamental issues. Orwell presents this in the arguments between Napoleon and Snowball. In particular Snowball believes in industrial progress (hence his plans for the windmill) and the conversion of the other farms to Animalism – Orwell's word for communism. Like Stalin, Napoleon believes in the greater importance of agriculture and the necessity of arming the country against attack from outside.

Such an attack does indeed come about. Not all the Soviet people accepted the communist revolution. The so-called White Russians in particular were opposed to it, and the Battle of the Cowshed represents the attacks of these forces of the counter-revolution against the Bolsheviks. The Bolsheviks eventually won, but just as Stalin forced Trotsky into exile, so Napoleon now forces Snowball off the farm. Far from there being a 'dictatorship of the proletariat' or rule by all the animals as equals, we increasingly see the dictatorship of Napoleon alone, just as Russia fell into the hands of Stalin alone.

A reign of terror begins on Animal Farm, just as it did in Russia. Orwell here presents three main aspects of Stalin's rule. First we are shown the terrible purges by which millions of Russians were sent to their deaths for alleged conspiracies against Stalin and sympathy with Trotsky. Secondly we are shown in Napoleon's negotiations with Frederick and Pilkington an equivalent of Stalin's devious dealings with Germany and Britain. Just as these led, after a phoney non-aggression pact, to Hitler's invasion of Eastern Europe, so when Napoleon has been duped into selling Frederick a pile of wood, which is paid for in counterfeit money, Frederick himself invades the farm. Although Frederick is expelled (just as Hitler was at the Battle of Stalingrad) he manages to destroy the windmill that the animals were building. The building of the windmill represents the third aspect of Stalin's rule in Russia that Orwell draws our attention to: the so-called Five-Year Plan by which the backward Russian economy was to be placed on a modern foundation. In both Russia and Animal Farm this required enormous labour and great suffering. It was also severely set back by the invasion of Hitler.

Just as Stalin became increasingly obsessed with the power of his own position, so does Napoleon. He awards himself medals, is given ridiculous titles and, when he appears in public, is surrounded by pomp. Far worse, on each step of his rise to power he breaks one of the Seven Commandments of Animalism which the pigs created from old Major's speech. In showing this, Orwell suggests how Stalin in his rise to power overturned all the ideals that originally underlay the communist revolution. To achieve this the lies of propaganda were essential, and Orwell shows, in the figure of Squealer, the grip that such propaganda had on the Russian people.

The ultimate betrayal comes at the end of the last chapter. Napoleon is shown conversing with the human beings – the original capitalists – and he is indistinguishable from them. The principles of Animalism have been wholly betrayed. This is the way in which Orwell shows he believed that the original principles of communism were finally betrayed by Stalin at the Tehran Conference when, with Churchill and the American president Roosevelt, he formed an alliance, which, Orwell supposed, was designed to carve up the world. None the less, the row that breaks out between Napoleon and the human beings also suggests the coming of the Cold War or the long period of hatred between Russia and the West. Orwell thus shows at the end of his book how the communist leader has become no better than the capitalists he replaced. *Animal Farm* is a grim meditation on how revolutions are betrayed from within, on how the ideal of freedom can become a nightmare, a hell on earth. Once all the animals were equal. Now some are 'more equal' than others. The old injustices triumph. Nothing has really changed. The revolution has been for nothing.

Synopsis

Animal Farm is an allegory. This means that under the surface of the story there is another level of meaning. This deeper level concerns one of the greatest events of modern times: the communist revolution in Russia (see pp. 6–9). Characters and events in Orwell's story thus correspond to characters and events in world history. Here we will briefly outline the relationship between these two levels. This will give us an overview of the whole novel and so a basis on which to build more detailed observations.

Having made a half-hearted attempt to lock up his animals for the night, Farmer Jones goes to bed drunk. In his inefficient and sometimes cruel management of Manor Farm we can begin to see Jones as a figure representing Orwell's view of capitalism. Capitalists profit from the labour of others, just as Jones profits from his animals. In particular Jones represents the old Russian aristocracy and, more specifically, the Russian Tsar or emperor. It was the Tsar's form of government, which cruelly exploited ordinary working people, that the Russian communists or Bolsheviks wished to overthrow. In this they were inspired by two men: Karl Marx and Vladimir Ilyich Lenin.

In Orwell's novel Marx and Lenin are represented by the figure of Major, the old white boar. We learn that Major has had a dream and that he wants to tell the rest of the animals about it. When Jones has fallen asleep, the animals gather in the barn to hear what Major has to say.

As the animals enter and settle down, so we are introduced to the main characters in the book. Note the skilful way in which Orwell describes them. They are all very definitely animals, but we feel for them as we might for human beings. By stirring our sympathy in this way Orwell makes his individual animals appeal to our emotions. Because they appeal to our emotions, we are hurt and angered by what happens to them in the revolution. The basis of Orwell's exposure of communism is thus an appeal to human sympathy. This leads eventually to a sense of outrage as the leaders of the revolution betray its high ideals and cause suffering to the other animals.

The ideals of the revolution at first make a profound appeal to the reader's sympathy, though they are later shown to cause hell on earth. Major describes the animals' wretched existence in such vivid terms that the reader immediately understands why they want a revolution.

The animals' lives are hard and short. They are no more than slaves. Yet England is a rich and fertile country. Is it natural they should live unhappily like this? No. The reason for their miserable lives is the fact that the animals have been exploited by man, although man is much weaker than they are. Man can do little himself; he has to use the animals. He is dependent on them. In return, however, he treats them with the utmost cruelty, even slaughtering them if he chooses. Major declares that the only way of throwing off such gross injustice is rebellion. The rule of man must be done away with. The animals must be their own masters. All the food they produce will then be theirs. They will own what they have worked for. Revolution will make them free – or so it seems.

Orwell is here portraying a central idea of communism: the belief that just as Jones's animals are exploited by a figure weaker than themselves, so the mass of ordinary working people are exploited by the forces of capitalism. According to this view the capitalists do very little work themselves, yet they own everything. In particular they own the labour of ordinary people – the proletariat. Marx believed that only by ousting the capitalists would the proletariat be free to enjoy what they themselves produced. And just as old Major thinks that such a revolution is bound to come about one day because there are so many animals and they are so much stronger than Jones, so Marx and his followers believed that ordinary men and women would one day assert their power and throw off the rule of the capitalists. Major ends the first part of his speech with a rosy vision of all animals as equals – comrades united in revolution.

But Orwell goes on to show how and why revolutions are so often betrayed from within. Neither men nor animals can live up to the high ideals of Marx, Lenin and Major. For example, Major has no sooner stopped urging love and equality on his audience than the dogs chase the rats to their holes. The old, natural cruelties will always exist. For all its appeal to freedom, brotherhood, and equality, Major's dream is just that – a dream, an illusion. On the farm this dream of freedom will turn into a nightmare. The same thing happened in Stalin's Russia.

Orwell helps us to measure just how completely the revolution is betrayed. When the rumpus caused by the dogs and rats has been silenced, old Major outlines in detail the ideals by which the animals should live. Each of these ideals will be destroyed.

Major declares that since man is the enemy and has two legs, all four-legged animals or animals with wings must be 'comrades'. The animals must fight constantly against man but never come to resemble him. They must not live in houses, sleep in beds, wear clothes, drink alcohol, smoke, handle money or engage in trade. No animal must ever tyrannize another. No animal must kill another. The tragic irony of *Animal Farm* lies in the fact that each of these ideals is warped and overridden by the pigs as they establish their power. Major's dream becomes a nightmare indeed.

Major tells the assembled animals of a long-forgotten song he has been reminded of by his dream. This song is called 'Beasts of England' and is the animal's version of 'The Internationale', the battle hymn of revolutionaries across the world. The song promises a future golden time when man has been overthrown. It expresses all the fervour and idealism of revolution. The song will encourage the animals when events go against them. Eventually the pigs will decree that it should no more be sung.

But, for the moment, all the beasts sing as well as they can, performing the song no less than five times. This creates such a din that Jones is wakened. He believes a fox has got into the farm and that his livestock is in danger. He does not realize that the animals are preparing to overthrow him. Just as the Tsar silenced early revolutionaries in Russia with gunshot, so Jones manages to silence the animals here. His victory will not last for long, however. He will not have many more nights in Manor Farm.

Old Major dies but his ideas live on in others. Trusting to his dream of revolution the animals begin a programme of education to prepare themselves for the glorious day of freedom. The pigs take the lead in this, just as in Russia, where Bolshevik or communist thinkers took the lead in educating the proletariat.

The pigs are the most intelligent animals on the farm, and two of them now emerge as the leaders. Knowledge, it seems, is power. The first pig is Napoleon. He is named by Orwell after the French emperor who began as a revolutionary and ended as a tyrant. In the allegory Napoleon represents the communist leader Stalin, who was also a tyrant. Through his chief pig's name Orwell seems to suggest that revolutionary leaders end up as oppressors and that revolutions are betrayed by their initiators.

Napoleon is large, fierce and devious. Snowball, his companion, is quicker witted, but not so strong a character. In the allegory Snowball represents Trotsky. A fuller account of the real Stalin and Trotsky can be found on pp. 6–9.

Napoleon and Snowball are helped in their plans by a third pig: Squealer. Squealer's name and his brilliant twisting of other animals' arguments suggest that he is a master of propaganda. Propaganda is the means by which a political party tries to show it is always right. This usually involves lies and distortions. To the pigs – Napoleon in particular – propaganda is essential to power. And power means corruption. In the course of *Animal Farm* all Major's high ideals will be twisted to their own advantage by the pigs, with the help of Squealer's propaganda. The revolution, begun in idealism, will be sustained by lies.

Many of the animals do not understand the real nature of the revolution, however. This is particularly true of Mollie. Mollie represents the White Russians – the counter-revolutionary forces loyal to the Tsar – and she longs for the luxuries only capitalist man can give her.

Moses the raven (one of Mr Jones's favoured pets) tells everyone of a never-never-land called Sugarcandy Mountain, to which all the animals will go after death. Sugarcandy Mountain, of course, is heaven. Moses thus represents the Russian Orthodox Church, which the Bolsheviks saw as an enemy to the revolution. For Marx all religion was 'the opiate of the people'. It drugged them into a stupid acceptance of life and so prevented them from thinking for themselves.

The pigs' most faithful followers are Boxer and Clover, the representatives of the proletariat or ordinary working people. In Chapter One Boxer is shown as strong and kindly but rather stupid. He is unfailingly loyal, however, even though he cannot make out the full implications of what the pigs tell him. Boxer thus represents the ordinary working man trapped in the deceits of his communist masters.

The revolution itself comes about more quickly than any of the animals expected. Jones has been drinking more and more and neglects his farm. In other words, the capitalists are undone by their own weaknesses. Eventually Jones forgets even to feed his animals, and the animals turn on him and his helpers, driving them from the farm. In the same way the Russian proletariat revolted at food shortages in 1917 and found that they had overthrown the forces of the Tsar. Mrs Jones (the Tsarina) also flees the farm and is followed by Moses the raven. Moses, however, will return.

The animals rejoice in their new freedom and destroy the cruel instruments Jones once used to oppress them. The ribbons that so delighted Mollie are also burned. They are considered as clothes, and Major had shown that clothes are corrupting, human things. Hearing this the foolishly loyal Boxer throws his useful sun-hat on the fire. Having once again expressed their joy, the animals return to the farm buildings. At first they are scared to enter them, but Napoleon and Snowball force their way in. Once again the pigs emerge as the natural leaders.

Just as the Russian revolutionaries who stormed the Winter Palace of the Tsar were amazed at the riches they found there, so the animals are awestruck by the wealth of Mr Jones. For true revolutionaries, of course, the pictures and furniture in Manor Farm are the corrupt trappings of capitalism. Mollie, however, is still deeply attached to such things and is reproached for her vanity. The irony lies in the fact that the pigs – the so-called revolutionaries – are also attracted to these trappings of capitalism. Despite old Major's warnings, by the close of the novel the pigs will end up as the masters of the farm, will live in its buildings, enjoy its luxuries and seem indistinguishable from the humans who once owned it.

But for now, in the fervour of revolt, the name of the farm is changed from Manor Farm to Animal Farm. In just the same way the empire of Russia became the Union of Soviet Socialist Republics. The last and damning irony will come when the pigs, associating with the humans, change the name of the farm back to its original. The revolution will have been wholly betrayed.

In the meantime the Seven Commandments of 'Animalism' – Orwell's name, in the book, for communism – are inscribed in huge letters on the barn wall. These commandments are the rules once set out by Major in his speech. They now become the Animalist manifesto – the central ideas of Animalist thinking. Each of these seven ideals will in turn be perverted and eventually destroyed by the pigs. In presenting this, Orwell shows the depth of the corruption wrought by the pigs as they turn democracy into tyranny.

The end of Chapter Two already suggests that it is the pigs who will work the corruption of the revolution. We are told that the cows need milking. It was promised by old Major that after the revolution the calves would enjoy all their mothers' milk. Now, however, as Napoleon sends the other animals off to work, we are told that on their return the milk has 'disappeared'. The milk is a luxury stolen by the pigs from the very workers who produced it. The revolution is indeed being corrupted from within.

The opening of Chapter Three shows the first apparently glorious days of the revolution. Nearly every animal works as hard as it can and many take Boxer as their shining example of true Animalism. 'I will work harder' is both Boxer's motto and theirs. As a result the harvests are abundant. There is food for all. Mollie and the cat shirk their responsibilities, however, while Benjamin the cynical donkey refuses to be excited. He has lived too long to believe that life is easily changed for the better.

On Sundays there is no work on the farm. The Animalist green flag is raised and a meeting is held to discuss future projects. The pigs are completely in charge of these meetings, where the enmity between Napoleon and Snowball soon becomes clear.

The pigs have been studying hard, and Snowball in particular is keen to set up all sorts of planning committees to improve the animals' way of life. However, with the exception of the education committees, all these projects fail.

The stupider animals cannot learn to read and are unable even to memorize the Seven Commandments. The pigs take advantage of this and simplify the commandments down to one crude rule: 'Four legs good, two legs bad'. This becomes a meaningless slogan chanted by the sheep when anything goes wrong.

We also learn that the dogs have had pups. Right at the start it was shown that the dogs were somewhat ambitious animals akin to the pigs. Now their pups are taken away by Napoleon. For a while this raises no suspicion. Only later do we learn that these puppies have been trained as Napoleon's fearful personal police force, the equivalent of Stalin's secret police.

Note how subtly Orwell portrays Napoleon's evil mind at work. Throughout the first half of the novel we are given strong clues to his evil intentions, but only after the expulsion of Snowball (which he has been planning all along) do these become clear. We are dupes of his plot almost as much as the animals are.

It is decreed that the windfall apples should be reserved for the pigs alone. As they have already commandeered the milk supplies, the other animals are considerably upset by this and the pigs are forced to send out their propaganda agent to quieten them down. Squealer tells the animals that the pigs have reserved the apples not because they like them but because eating them is essential for preserving their health. Good health is necessary for animals involved in so much brain-work. And that work, in turn, is essential if Jones is not to return. None of the animals would want that, would they? The animals are won over by Squealer's propaganda. The pigs get their way. The road to tyranny seems clear.

News of the animals' rebellion has spread. This is due partly to the efforts of the pigs, who have sent flights of pigeons off over neighbouring areas, just as the Bolsheviks sent agents out to promote their activities. Many of the animals across England find the news of the rebellion deeply comforting. This is despite the fact that the local farmers have circulated false rumours of appalling crimes practised on Animal Farm. This again corresponds to the rumours about life in communist Russia circulated by the great European powers. Among these European powers were Britain and Germany. In the novel, Britain is represented by Foxwood Farm, and its owner, Mr Pilkington, stands for Churchill; Pinchfield Farm and its proprietor Mr Frederick stand for Germany and Hitler.

Pilkingon and Frederick are suspicious of each other. Neither wishes actively to help Jones at first. Eventually, however, they join forces to attack Animal Farm in what becomes known as the Battle of the Cowshed.

The battle has long been expected by Snowball, who has prepared for such an invasion by the forces of the 'counter-revolution'. Orwell brilliantly describes the animals' first attack, their tactical retreat and final onslaught. Note that Snowball himself plays a brave and conspicuous part in this, while Napoleon is not mentioned. Later Napoleon will use the battle as propaganda for his own twisted purposes.

Mollie also takes little part in the battle. She is frightened, and her sympathies are really with the enemy. Boxer fights with particular strength, but is greatly upset when he thinks he has killed a stable-lad. Something of Snowball's hardness is revealed when he tells Boxer that the only good human is a dead one.

There is an excited victory celebration after the battle. The one sheep that died is given an honourable burial. Snowball is awarded a military decoration for his conspicuous bravery. A war memorial is erected and it is decreed that the anniversaries of the battle and the rebellion will be celebrated.

At the start of Chapter Five we learn that Mollie has been shirking. Worse, Clover has spotted her with one of Mr Pilkington's men, whom she allowed to stroke her nose. Mollie half-heartedly denies this, but Clover finds sugar and ribbons hidden in Mollie's stall, which only a human could have given her. Three days later Mollie disappears, to be seen a while afterwards harnessed between the shafts of a dogcart in the nearby town. Mollie has betrayed the principles of Animalism and gone over to the humans. In terms of the allegory the White Russians have defected to the capitalists. Mollie is never mentioned by the animals again.

As in the communist Politburo the pigs now make all the decisions on the farm, though these decisions have to be agreed by a majority vote at the Sunday Meetings. These meetings also reveal increasingly strong disagreements between Napoleon and Snowball, both of whom are competing for leadership like Stalin and Trotsky. Napoleon, emerging as an ever more sinister figure, has trained the sheep to interrupt Snowball's inspired speeches by bleating out their slogan: 'Four legs good, two legs bad'.

Matters between Napoleon and Snowball come to a head over the building of the windmill. In terms of the allegory, this project represents Russia's move towards industrialization, or the attempt to modernize her means of manufacture. This movement was first led by Trotsky but was opposed by Stalin.

Snowball has visions of a technological future that will help reduce the workers' burdens. He works hard on his designs for the windmill, which will be the farm's source of industrial power. Napoleon, in his carefully contrived contempt for Snowball, merely urinates on his plans. Like Stalin, he apparently prefers agricultural improvement to industrial advance.

The disagreement leads to bitter divisions among the other animals. These are aggravated by a second conflict, which concerns the defence of the farm. Napoleon, like Stalin, believes his first duty is to build up a strong home base. Snowball, like Trotsky, believes that if all the neighbouring farms are converted to Animalism, then they will have no enemies to defend themselves against.

The crisis comes at a Sunday Meeting. Indeed, this is the central moment in the novel. Up to this point an appearance at least of democracy and debate has been maintained on Animal Farm. When Napoleon and his private police expel Snowball, however, this pretence is no longer necessary. Just as Stalin became the dictator of Russia, ruling the state with the increasing insanity of a despot, so now Napoleon becomes the undisputed master of Animal Farm, ruling it with deviousness, cruelty and blatant hypocrisy. The dream of freedom is lost, and a long night of suffering opens before the helpless animals as their revolution is betrayed.

So far we have seen Snowball as an energetic, brave and comparitively open leader and one keen to advance the welfare of the farm. Napoleon, by contrast, has shown himself less obvious in his actions, more suspicious. He has been biding his time. Now, at the Sunday Meeting, as Snowball sings the praises of his plan for the windmill, Napoleon realizes his time has come. When all the animals have been carried away by Snowball's eloquence, Napoleon plays the evil gambit by which he secures what he always wanted: absolute power. As the animals bask in Snowball's dream, Napoleon utters a strange, high-pitched sound and his secretly trained police come running in. They chase Snowball out of the barn, across the farm and beyond its hedges.

Napoleon's reign of terror begins immediately. Surrounded by his dogs, Napoleon tells the animals that all debate on the farm will cease. A special pig committee will make every necessary decision.

Even Boxer is troubled by this, but Squealer explains matters away and begins the process of discrediting Snowball's part in events. Propaganda and lies are at work in a despotic or totalitarian state.

Boxer is taken in by these lies and adopts as his second motto the phrase 'Napoleon is always right'.

Napoleon now declares that the windmill will be built after all. This will mean hard work and even reduced rations. Since Napoleon had at first opposed the building of the windmill, it requires all of Squealer's abilities to convince the animals of the sincerity his motives. Squealer's explanations, however, manage to present Napoleon as the pig with the animals' interests most at heart, while Snowball appears as the enemy.

The animals work extremely hard at building the windmill. In terms of the allegory this project represents Stalin's first and unsuccessful Five-Year Plan by which he hoped to modernize Russia. Napoleon encourages the animals to give up their Sunday afternoons to the labour of building the windmill with the threat that their rations will be halved if they do not. Building the windmill proves very difficult, but the animals manage to solve many of the problems that arise through sheer hard work and ingenuity. Boxer, in particular, is an example of selfless labour.

Because of all the work on the windmill, Animal Farm suffers from various shortages of essential supplies. The animals also need various tools and pieces of machinery. They are unsure how they will get these since they cannot make them themselves.

Napoleon has an answer to this – and his answer is yet another betrayal of the principles of Animalism. The farm will engage in trade with the outside world. This in turn means handling money and bargaining with human beings. All these activities were prohibited by old Major. All of them were written up on the barn wall as examples of things the animals should never do. Once again we see the revolution being betrayed from within.

To pay for human goods, Napoleon requires that the chickens sacrifice their eggs. These will be sold to raise money. Napoleon has already made all the arrangements with the outside world. A local solicitor, Mr Whymper, will act as his go-between.

The animals are made uneasy by this, but once again Squealer is sent out to pacify them with propaganda. The sight of Napoleon dealing with Mr Whymper also gives them some satisfaction. We are told that the outside world is still somewhat hostile to Animal Farm and is hoping it will go bankrupt.

The pigs now begin to pervert yet more of the original principles of

Animalism. They start to live inside the farmhouse, eat in it and even sleep in its beds. Clover and Muriel are suspicious and they go to consult the original ideals of Animalism painted on the barn wall. They discover that the commandments have been very subtly changed. The rule that no animal should sleep in a bed has been altered to read that no animal should sleep in a bed 'with sheets'. The principles of Animalism are being undermined, and this is being concealed by lies and Squealer's propaganda.

By November – and as a result of intense labour – the windmill is half finished. One night it is blown down in a terrible storm. The animals are reduced to near despair, but Napoleon immediately takes charge of the situation. He declares that the entire responsibility for the collapse of the windmill lies with Snowball, who, as an enemy of the people, has sabotaged the building.

Work on rebuilding the windmill begins at once, though this causes considerable suffering. Food shortages occur (just as they did in communist Russia), and the animals face starvation. Napoleon tries to hide the worst effects from the outside world.

Once again the chickens are told to surrender their eggs. They protest at this and smash them, just as the Russian peasantry ruined their farms when they were told that the communists wished to take them over. Animal Farm is near to rebellion. Napoleon ruthlessly crushes all opposition, however, just as Stalin was to do in Russia.

There is also a large supply of timber on the farm that Napoleon realizes he can sell. For a while he plays Mr Pilkington off against Mr Frederick as they try to buy this timber.

Meanwhile rumours of Snowball's return are circulated and everything that goes wrong on the farm is attributed to his sabotage. Napoleon makes Snowball's activities seem so rampant that a reign of terror is established. Lies become the language of the day. Napoleon declares that Snowball was in league with Mr Jones all the time and that the Battle of the Cowshed was Snowball's attempt to put Jones back in power. Nothing could be further from the truth, but in this totalitarian state the truth seems hardly to matter any more.

Even Boxer finds these accusations by the pigs difficult to accept, and it takes all Squealer's powers of persuasion to convince him that black is white.

Stalin eliminated all opposition in Russia through a terrible series of 'purges'. These were state trials in which anyone showing the least trace of opposition was wiped out. It is estimated that Stalin himself signed over 44,000 death warrants for men, women and even children. In *Animal Farm* a similar series of show trials now takes place. Some of the pigs confess that they have been in contact with Snowball. They add that Snowball acted as Jones's secret agent. After the pigs' confessions their throats are torn out by Napoleon's dogs. Three hens, a goose and some sheep then confess to similar crimes. Few, if any, of these crimes have actually been committed, but in the atmosphere of hysterical terror Napoleon has created the animals will confess to anything. Similarly in Stalin's Russia innocent victims would confess to any crime.

Another principle of Animalism has now been destroyed. Animals are killing each other. Those animals who survive realize painfully how far their revolution has been destroyed. To raise their spirits they begin to sing 'Beasts of England'. As they are singing it for a third time, Squealer and the dogs approach and tell them that the song has been banned. A far less powerful song is substituted for the original battle hymn.

At the start of Chapter Eight the animals discover that the Sixth Commandment has been altered. It is no longer forbidden for an animal to kill another; instead no animal must kill another 'without cause'. Meanwhile the remaining animals work incredibly hard and are fed with false statistics about the success of the farm.

Napoleon is becoming an increasingly remote leader, obsessed with the outward trappings of power. He is also conducting a series of devious negotiations with the neighbouring farms. In the same way, before the outbreak of the Second World War, Stalin began a series of complex discussions with the West, eventually signing a pact with Germany, just as Napoleon reaches an agreement with Frederick.

At first Frederick is presented as an enemy in league with Snowball, and terrible rumours are circulated of his cruelty. Further show trials take place on Animal Farm. Meanwhile the windmill is finished. The animals are very proud of its apparent strength, and it is declared that the windmill will be named Napoleon Mill.

Then, quite arbitrarily, the animals are told that the timber is to be sold to Frederick. By appearing to be friendly with Pilkington, Napoleon has forced Frederick to raise his price for the timber. To many of the pigs this seems a masterpiece of skilful negotiation. Napoleon has also demanded payment in cash rather than by cheque. When the timber is eventually paid for, however, the notes are discovered to be forgeries. Just as Stalin's negotiations with Hitler ended with Germany's invasion of Russia, so Napoleon's negotiations with Frederick result in deceit and the eventual invasion of Animal Farm.

Frederick's forces invade with every appearance of success. They get right to the heart of the farm and even surround the windmill. In the same way Hitler's troops invaded deep into the heart of Russia. And just as devastation was caused to Russian industry by Hitler's attack, so the forces of Frederick contrive to blow up the windmill.

The animals retaliate with all the bravery at their command, just as the Russian people made enormous sacrifices at the Battle of Stalingrad to keep the enemy Germans at bay. Losses are incurred on both sides, but eventually Frederick's men are forced to withdraw.

The devastation left on the farm is appalling, and the fact that the stones of the mill have been smashed and scattered makes rebuilding all but impossible. Boxer in particular, wounded in the battle, sees what a monumental task this will be. None the less a celebration is called for and the animals' spirits are raised. A great funeral is held for the dead.

The pigs now discover whisky. Previously it had been one of the cardinal rules of Animalism that no animal should imitate man by drinking alcohol. However, the pigs get disgustingly drunk (Napoleon even wears a bowler hat, thereby identifying himself even more strongly with the humans) and the hangovers they suffer are so bad that it is given out that Napoleon is dying. However, he recovers and immediately starts taking an interest in brewing. Part of the farm is set aside to grow crops to be turned into alcohol for the pigs. At the close of the chapter another of the principles of Animalism is subtly perverted by Squealer and the pigs. It is declared that far from no animal being allowed to drink alcohol, from now on no animal will be allowed to drink it 'to excess'.

Boxer sustained a split hoof in the battle and this takes a long time to heal. Despite his being old, and the fact that he should soon be allowed to retire, according to the original laws of Animal Farm, Boxer continues working with his old enthusiasm. Meanwhile life on the farm is hard. Rations are reduced. The animals none the less continue to believe the false statistics issued by Squealer about the success of the farm. More sacrifices are called for, particularly to build a school for Napoleon's children.

The pigs live a life of luxury in the farmhouse (where they also drink the alcohol they have learned to brew) while the rest of the animals have to stand the chill and dark of winter. So-called 'Spontaneous Demonstrations' are held to keep up the animals' spirits, and Napoleon is elected president of the republic of Animal Farm.

In the spring Moses the Raven returns after an absence of several years and is allowed to remain on the farm. In the allegory this represents Stalin's attempts to come to an agreement with the church. This was regarded with universal contempt and earned Stalin much criticism in the West. Many of the animals begin to believe in Moses's stories of Sugarcandy Mountain. After all, life is so hard on the farm that it is some comfort to believe in a better existence after death.

Boxer's hoof begins to heal. Despite his being almost twelve years old he continues to work as hard as ever. Eventually, however, he collapses. The animals at once rush to his aid and then fetch Squealer. Clover, meanwhile, attends to Boxer. Squealer returns saying that Napoleon has arranged for Boxer to be taken to hospital in the nearby town of Willingdon. For two days, whenever they are not working in the fields, Benjamin and Clover attend Boxer as he lies in his stall.

It is Benjamin who notices that Boxer is being taken away. This is one of the cruellest and most moving scenes in the whole book. It is the moment that finally convinces us – if we still need convincing – of the utter ruthlessness of Napoleon, and of his complete disregard for any sort of decency at all. It is not an animal ambulance that has come to take Boxer away; he is not being sent to hospital. The vehicle that arrives is a knacker's van. The sickly Boxer has been sold for what his meat will fetch. Eventually the animals realize this, but it is too late. They desperately call out to Boxer to save himself. Once he would have been strong enough to smash the van to smithereens. Now he can only kick ineffectively at its sides. Boxer is never seen again.

Squealer's propaganda now becomes particularly revolting. He gives an entirely false picture of the care lavished on Boxer in his final hours and suppresses any idea that the horse has been dragged away to the knacker's yard. Surely, he says, the animals know better than to think that Napoleon would behave like that. Eventually they agree. They have been wholly taken in by propaganda and lies. All of the animals are merely Napoleon's dupes. They do not even realize that Napoleon spends the money raised from Boxer's meat on whisky. So much for the idealism of revolution. The animal who worked the hardest, who was the most loyal and the most unquestioning, is sold off for a few bottles of alcohol. It is a terrible moment.

But worse is to come – the final and complete betrayal of the animals' revolution.

Years have passed and many of the animals have died. The farm is now comparatively prosperous. However, the rebuilt windmill is used for grinding corn for profit, and the ease that Snowball had planned it would bring to the animals' lives is not seen. Indeed, luxury is declared to be contrary to the spirit of Animalism. Few of the animals can remember the bad old days when the farm was owned by Jones and so have nothing with which to compare the present. To them Napoleon's rule seems the natural way of things. It does not appear wrong that all the luxuries go to the pigs who do no useful or real work.

Despite their hard life and all the injustices, the animals never give up hope. After all, theirs is the only farm in England run entirely by animals, and this in itself is something to be proud of. They even believe that the great day of freedom will soon come. They still think all animals are equal.

They are to be horribly betrayed. Our suspicions are first aroused when the foolish sheep are taken out by Napoleon and Squealer and given secret instruction. Later the pigs are to be seen walking round the farm on their hind legs. Napoleon even carries a whip in his trotter. The rest of the animals are absolutely appalled. Then the stupid sheep strike up the new chorus they have been taught. In the past, four legs had been good and two legs bad. Now there is a new mindless chant: Four legs are good but two legs are even better!

When Clover persuades Benjamin to read to her the commandments on the barn wall, we see just how far the revolution has been betrayed. In place of the seven rules that had once defined the spirit of Animalism there is now only one amended commandment:

ALL ANIMALS ARE EQUAL
BUT SOME ANIMALS ARE MORE
EQUAL THAN OTHERS

The revolution has been wholly betrayed, and it comes as little suprise when the pigs are seen wearing human clothes, reading human magazines and receiving parties of neighbouring human beings with whom they discuss business matters.

Once the humans were the enemy. They were the capitalists, the people who exploited the animals on the farm for their own profit. But the great revolution that resulted in the humans being defeated and expelled has now come full circle. The pigs are as exploitative as the humans were – perhaps more so. Napoleon himself is completely at one with the old enemy. As the rest of the animals gather round the farm windows, they see a disgusting sight: pigs and humans are talking together as if there were no differences between them. They are all drunk, all corrupt, all compromising. As Napoleon reveals that the farm is now the property of the pigs, he also declares that he will change its name back to Manor Farm. It is as if the revolution had never been.

The other animals look on appalled. Although quarrels soon break out between the pigs and the humans (in terms of the allegory this represents the cooling of relations between Russia and the West), as the animals stare in through the window they can see no difference between pigs and men, communists and capitalists. It is a bleak and terrible ending. The revolution and all the suffering that went with it were for nothing. One tyranny has merely been replaced by another.

Chapter-by-chapter Analysis

CHAPTER ONE

Farmer Jones has been drinking. We are told that he has made the rounds of Manor Farm to lock up the animals for the night, but that he has failed to do this properly. He returns to the farmhouse, has a last glass of beer and then goes to bed, leaving the farm to the animals.

There has been much talk among the animals. They have heard that old Major, a prize-winning and highly respected boar, has something he wishes to tell them. As soon as Jones is asleep and the farm is theirs, the animals gather in the barn. Note the delicacy and affection with which Orwell describes the animals as they enter the barn and settle down to hear what Major has to say. Orwell makes us aware that his animals are real farmyard creatures and yet they are also beasts with thoughts and feelings with which we can identify.

For example, old Major is stout, majestic, wise and kindly in appearance. Clearly he is a figure of some standing for whom the animals have respect. Notice also the subtle manner in which Orwell's description of the animals points to the way in which the characters will develop. For example, the first animals that enter are the dogs and the pigs. For the moment it seems perfectly natural that these intelligent animals should take their place at the front of the audience. Only later do we come to see the pigs as ruthlessly ambitious animals and the dogs as their cruel and devoted servants.

A wealth of other farm animals now enters: hens, pigeons, sheep and cows. We are also introduced to the two cart-horses, Boxer and Clover. In the political allegory that underlies *Animal Farm* Boxer and Clover represent the ordinary working people – the proletariat. Orwell describes them with both tenderness and shrewd under-

standing. He never lets his descriptions slide into mawkish senti-
mentality.

We see the enormous size of Boxer and Clover. We guess their
immense strength, but we see also their natural kindness and delicacy.
They are very careful to place their hooves so as to avoid any small
animals that might be hidden in the straw.

Clover is the stout and motherly cart-horse. We are told that Boxer
is an enormous beast and as strong as two ordinary horses. However,
he has a somewhat stupid look about him, and Orwell tells us that
while he is not a creature of the greatest intelligence, he is widely
respected for his steady character and ability to work hard. These are
the qualities that will characterize Boxer throughout. We will see him
as kind and gentle, unfailingly loyal, immensely hard-working but
quite unable to see the true evil of the pigs. The pigs become his
masters and eventually sell him off to the knacker's yard, spending
the money they get on whisky.

We are deeply sympathetic to Boxer, despite his obvious limitations.
The fact that he is so cruelly betrayed by the pigs rouses our anger to
such an extent that we are made to feel how ruthless the power-
seeking pigs really are. One of the ways in which Orwell makes us
realize the true evil of Soviet communism is by making this appeal to
our feelings of compassion and arousing our anger.

We are also introduced to other animals: Muriel the white goat and
Benjamin the donkey. Benjamin is an important character. Orwell's
novel is concerned with the betrayal of the revolution, with the way in
which ideals of liberty are corrupted by those who seek power for its
own sake. This is a grim and bitter view. Most of the animals have
high hopes for the revolution at the start of the book and only in the
later chapters do we see their progressive disillusion. Benjamin,
however, is doubtful from the start. He says donkeys live longer
than other animals and so see more of the world and its disappoint-
ments.

In fact Benjamin is something of a cynic. Although he takes part
in the revolution, he never really believes that its aims will improve
the animals' lives. Right from the start of the book Benjamin is the
voice warning us that things may well not turn out as happily as we
expect. None the less, for all his cynicism, Benjamin is devoted to
Boxer. In other words, he has a deep sympathy with the hard life of

ordinary working people. Perhaps, in some respects, we can see Benjamin as a figure representing Orwell himself: a man deeply sympathetic to the sufferings of ordinary people, yet too shrewd and worldly wise to believe that revolutions are necessarily a good thing.

Other animals also enter the barn. Among these is Mollie. Mollie is a vain and foolish white mare, a favourite of Mr Jones's and an animal who enjoys all the little luxuries humankind can give her. Mollie also has an important place in the political allegory that underlies *Animal Farm*. She represents the White Russians – those people who were opposed to the communist revolution in Russia and who sided with the forces of the Czar. Mollie, too, is never really a true part of the revolution, and she will eventually leave the farm to work alongside the human beings who give her the little treats she so desires.

Other animals, too, will have little part to play in the revolution. The cat, for example, is interested only in its own comfort, while Moses the tame raven (who, as we have seen, represents the Russian Orthodox Church) is also unsympathetic to the animals' cause.

Once the animals have all gathered and settled down, Major begins his speech. The charm and the detailed description with which Orwell opens his novel now give way to serious political comment.

Major's speech is a simple and powerful depiction of the ideals that underlie the communist philosophy of Marx and Lenin. Note the deft way in which Orwell introduces these ideas. He is not going to preach a difficult lesson. Rather he is going to introduce these ideas to us through our imaginations, through the power, passion and authority with which Major speaks.

Major wins immediate respectful attention by saying, first of all, that he believes that he is about to die. He wishes to pass on to the other animals his experience of life's problems and his proposed solutions.

First of all he offers a powerful description of the suffering that is the lot of the ordinary farmyard animal. He declares that their lives are 'miserable, laborious, and short'. The animals are given barely enough food. They are forced to work themselves to exhaustion until they are no longer wanted, and then they are slaughtered in the cruellest way. Major declares that no animal in England is either happy or free.

Major then asks an important question: Is the animals' life of slavery natural and inevitable? His answer to this is a resounding 'No'. England is a rich and fertile country. Even the farm they are living on now could easily support far more animals than live there at present, and it could support them in a luxury they can barely imagine. Clearly something is very seriously wrong. What is the root of the problem? Major answers his own question with a single word: Man.

Man is the great exploiter of the animals. He consumes everything they produce while he himself produces nothing. He lords it over the animals, working them hard. He takes milk from the cows that should really go towards producing healthy calves. He takes the eggs the hens have laid and sells them rather than letting them hatch into chickens. Even Clover's foals — which should be the comfort of her old age — have been sold off to make money.

But life is worse than this. Very few of the animals are allowed to live their natural life span. Old Major has been lucky in this respect, but he says that the young pigs will be slaughtered and tells Boxer that on the day he loses his strength he will be sold to the knacker's yard.

Major has eloquently convinced both the animals and us of the injustices that they suffer. He sees the only answer to these as being a rebellion that will overthrow the rule of man. As far as he is concerned (and his thoughts on this point are similar to those of Karl Marx) the revolution is bound to come one day. The animals should give all their attention to preparing for it.

We know, of course, that this revolution does indeed take place on *Animal Farm*. We also know that it will be hideously betrayed. But notice the subtle irony Orwell introduces even into the opening sections of Major's speech.

The picture Major gives of the suffering of the animals is very strong, but when the animals take over the running of the farm, many of the old injustices will be continued by the pigs. For example, Major declares that the cows' milk should all be given to their calves rather than be taken by man. But when the pigs take over, Napoleon makes sure that the milk goes to him and the other pigs. Similarly, the hens will not be allowed to hatch their eggs. Instead the eggs will be sold off to raise money for the pigs' projects. Most cruelly of all, the fate that awaits Boxer under the tyranny of the pigs is exactly the same as that which awaits him under the tyranny of man.

For Major, man is indeed the enemy. In the political allegory of *Animal Farm* man represents the capitalists and the animals represent the ordinary working people. Marx believed that capitalists were an evil force who exploited poor people, working them very hard, paying them almost nothing and denying them the right to enjoy what they themselves had produced. Like Major, Marx believed that only a revolution would set the world to rights and allow justice for all people.

But Orwell immediately makes us wonder if this is really the case. Major has spoken very eloquently about justice and how all animals should be seen as comrades, as equals. But he no sooner pauses to draw breath than the dogs catch sight of four large rats and chase them to their holes. There is real and natural viciousness in the animal world and no amount of preaching will ever get rid of this.

In the allegory of *Animal Farm* the wild animals such as the rats represent the great mass of Russian peasants. It is now agreed by the farm animals that these creatures should have their place in the new world that the revolution will create, just as the Russian peasantry were given their place in the Russian Revolution.

Major's vision of a fairer world is very moral and very idealistic. He not only tells the animals what they must do to improve their lives, but also warns them of the things they must avoid if they are not to become like the exploiting humans they will one day replace. For example, they must never walk on two legs like man and must avoid his vices. They must never live in a house, sleep in a bed, wear clothes, drink alcohol, smoke, use money or engage in trade. It is a measure of the collapse of the revolution on Animal Farm that each of these rules is eventually twisted by the pigs to their own advantage. The pigs will tyrannize the other animals in precisely the way that Major wishes to avoid. They will kill their comrades with bloodthirsty ruthlessness. While they seem to support the idea that 'all animals are equal', they finally pervert even this rule and declare that 'some animals are more equal than others'. We thus see right at the start of the novel all the ideals of the revolution that its leaders will betray.

Having set out his political manifesto and convinced the animals of the necessity of revolution, Major now tells them of his dream and, more particularly, of a song that his dream has reminded him of. This song is called 'Beasts of England'. Allegorically the song is the equivalent of the rousing 'Internationale' – the battle cry of communist revolutionaries the world over. The song expresses the yearning for an ideal golden age when the animals will be free and able to enjoy the products of their labour.

All of the animals gathered in front of Major sing the song at the tops of their voices. Their imaginations are so fired that they sing it through five times. The great din this makes eventually wakes the drunken Mr Jones. He believes a fox has got into the farm and frightened the animals, and he shoots his gun to scare the fox away. Certainly this has the effect of making all the animals hurry back to their stalls, just as the firing squads of the Russian Tsars managed to silence opposition for a while. None the less the animals now know that the chance of a better future lies with them alone. Just as the Tsar was deposed by the communist or Bolshevik revolutionaries, so Mr Jones will soon be thrown off his farm by his animals.

CHAPTER TWO

Though Old Major dies, his ideas live on. The more intelligent animals particularly are keen to establish his teaching on a firm foundation. The pigs take the leading part in this, as they are by far the most intelligent of the animals. In terms of the political allegory of the novel the pigs represent the Bolshevik revolutionaries, who worked hard and in secret to make sure that the Russian Revolution would be a success when it eventually came.

In the first chapter Orwell quietly introduced the pigs without naming them, merely showing how they sat in the front row during Old Major's lecture. Now two pigs in particular emerge as characters in their own right: Napoleon and Snowball. The names Orwell gives these pigs are significant. They tell us a great deal about the allegorical role of the pigs in the novel.

Napoleon represents the Russian tyrant Stalin. Napoleon himself, you will remember, was a French emperor who began as a revolutionary and became an autocrat. Napoleon the pig will do just the same. Similarly Stalin came to power as a man representing a political system that was designed to give justice to working people everywhere, but became a tyrant of unbelievable cruelty and ruthlessness. What Orwell seems to be suggesting here is something basic to his whole way of thinking in *Animal Farm*: the idea that all revolutions begin in idealism and end in tyranny. Indeed, Orwell wrote that he believed revolutions were essentially a 'swindle'. In their early days they promised people heaven on earth, but they always ended up making their lives hell. The dream of freedom rapidly degenerates into a nightmare.

The other pig is Snowball. Snowball represents Stalin's great rival, the communist thinker Trotsky. As Stalin became more and obsessed with his own personal power and the belief that he had to liquidate any and every form of opposition, so it became an obsession with him to murder anybody who could be in any way accused of sympathizing with Trotsky. We will see Napoleon behaving in exactly the same way. But let us consider Snowball's name a little more carefully. It, too, has a symbolic meaning. Snow melts away and is seen no more. Just so Snowball disintegrates before the power of Napoleon and is eventually driven from the farm, never to be seen again.

We also learn some important details about the characters of Napoleon and Snowball. Orwell tells us that Snowball is lively and quick-witted but does not have the depth of character that Napoleon has. Napoleon is fierce and careful of his words, but we are told that he also has 'a reputation for getting his own way'. As the novel develops, these traits become more and more sinister as Napoleon begins to assume absolute power over the other animals.

We are also introduced to a third pig: Squealer. Squealer is the pig who is responsible for the rest of the pigs' propaganda. In other words, he is the figure who will persuade the animals that, regardless of what happens, the pigs are always right. To do this Squealer will use lies, phoney arguments, threats, indeed anything that will justify his masters' actions. Squealer is wholly indifferent to the truth and he will twist facts and language in any way he can. Orwell, as a writer, was deeply aware of how immoral this use of language was. He also knew how easily a quick-witted and fast-talking politician could bamboozle people with a few well-chosen lies. As we shall see, Orwell cared passionately about language and the fact that it should clearly and fairly present the truth. Squealer's propaganda was something that revolted Orwell to the very depths of his being, and throughout *Animal Farm* he is concerned to show the effects of lies and propaganda on the lives of ordinary working people. Squealer's very name implies his corrupt nature, while his little twinkling eyes, his fast talking and his skipping from side to side suggest his devious and unstable character.

These three pigs have worked hard at reducing Major's teachings to a number of simple rules. These they call the principles of Animalism. But many of the animals are either too stupid or too lazy to understand the true nature of the revolution. They seem to think that the injustice inflicted by Mr Jones is part of the natural order of things and that they would starve to death if he were removed. Others ask why they should bother about the revolution if it is going to take place after their death or will come about whether they work for it or not.

Just as the Bolsheviks in Russia had to work very hard to educate the ordinary people into some degree of political awareness, so the pigs have to work constantly to make the animals aware of the true nature of revolution. Even so, they do not always succeed. Just as the Bolsheviks failed to convert the White Russians to their way of thinking, so the pigs fail to persuade Mollie that the revolution will be to her advantage.

In addition to indifference and stupidity the pigs have a third enemy in the form of Moses, the tame raven. Like Mollie, Moses is one of Mr Jones's pets. In other words, the raven is on the side of the capitalists rather than the ordinary working people or proletariat. Allegorically Moses represents the Russian Orthodox Church. His constant talk of a never-never land called 'Sugarcandy Mountain' – a place of freedom and joy the animals will go to after their death – suggests how the Russian Church tried to persuade people that after their hard lives they would go to heaven. The Bolsheviks saw such talk as very dangerous to their cause. The Bolsheviks were atheists. They did not believe either in God or heaven. Rather they believed that man must put matters right in this world and not wait for the imaginary delights of the hereafter. Marx in particular believed that religion was 'the opiate of the people'. It stopped them thinking. It stopped them wanting to change things.

The pigs, none the less, have much success in converting the animals to Major's views. In particular Boxer and Clover become their devoted followers. Orwell shows how dangerous such unthinking loyalty is. He has already told us that Boxer and Clover are not particularly intelligent. He now reminds us of this and shows us how the two cart-horses (the ordinary working people) accept everything they are told without question. This is potentially very dangerous. Boxer and Clover become the dupes of the pigs. It is their unquestioning loyalty and willingness to work hard that allows the pigs to become the tyrants of Animal Farm. The limitations of the creatures the revolution was most designed to serve are the very things that lead to the utter betrayal of the revolution itself. This is one of the grimmest political points that Orwell makes in his book.

The revolution comes about sooner than anyone expected. Jones has fallen on evil days. He is drinking more and more and neglecting his farm. One midsummer's eve he gets so drunk that he fails to return to the farm until late in the evening, when he is too drunk to attend to the animals. The starving beasts erupt in spontaneous revolt, kicking down the doors and helping themselves to food. Jones and his men try to quell them, but the situation soon gets out of control and they are forced to flee. Mrs Jones, seeing what is going on, also leaves hurriedly and is followed by Moses the raven. Suddenly and quite unexpectedly the farm belongs to the animals.

In terms of the political allegory the animals' revolt corresponds to the ordinary Russian people's actions when, in 1917, faced with starvation, they rose up against the Czar and expelled him. What happened in communist Russia will now be shown to happen on a smaller scale on Animal Farm.

At first everything is joy and excitement. The animals canter about the fields to see that the human beings have really gone and then race to the farm buildings. Here all the cruel instruments with which Jones repressed them are destroyed. Bits, chains, knives and whips are all burned. So, too, are the ribbons with which the animals were degradingly dressed on market days. Snowball declares that ribbons are human things and therefore corrupt, and that no animal should wear clothes. Boxer, hearing this, loyally throws his useful sun-hat on to the fire.

The following morning the excited animals gambol all over the farm, enjoying their new-found freedom. Then they return to the farmhouse. All but Snowball and Napoleon are afraid to enter. The pigs, showing themselves to be born leaders, barge their way in.

Just as the Bolshevik revolutionaries were amazed at the wealth that they saw when they stormed the palace of the Russian Tsar, so the animals can scarcely believe the luxury in which Mr and Mrs Jones once used to live. For true revolutionaries, such luxuries are the trappings of corrupt capitalism and should be shunned. Mollie, however, is still deeply attracted to them. She is not a revolutionary at all.

The rest of the animals declare that the farmhouse should be made into a museum and that none of them should ever live there. Notice the nice detail of Boxer smashing the beer barrel in the scullery while the pigs see that the hams hanging in the kitchen are taken out for burial.

A meeting is called after breakfast and is addressed by Snowball. He reveals that the pigs have taught themselves to read. Napoleon sends for pots of paint, and Snowball (who is the best at writing) paints out the old name of the farm and replaces it with the proud new title: Animal Farm. Just as the old empire of Russia became the Union of Soviet Socialist Republics, so 'Animal Farm' proclaims who rules there now.

The animals then go off to the big barn, where Snowball inscribes the Seven Commandments of Animalism on the wall. These are the rules in which the pigs have encapsulated Major's teachings. These commandments declare that whatever goes on two legs is an enemy, that any animal with four legs or wings is a friend and that clothes, beds and alcohol are all denied the animals. The sixth commandment states that no animal shall kill another, while the seventh reads 'All animals are equal'. Some of the animals begin to learn the commandments by heart.

It is declared that the Seven Commandments of Animalism are unalterable laws, which all the beasts must obey for evermore. In the course of the novel each of the seven commandments will be altered and betrayed by the pigs. In this we see the progressive corruption of the revolution as it follows its downward course from high idealism to hell on earth. These are very serious matters, but note the light touch of humour with which Orwell shows that Snowball's writing skills are not quite perfect!

There is work to do if the farm is to be successful, and Snowball urges the animals to the hayfield. But the cows have not been milked for twenty-four hours and their udders are almost bursting. The pigs set about milking them. One of the animals asks what is going to happen to the milk. You may remember that old Major said that it should be given to the calves so that they would grow up strong and healthy. Napoleon, however, declares that the animals should not worry their heads about the milk, the harvest is more important. When the animals return from the fields, they notice that the milk has 'disappeared'. Clearly it has been stolen by Napoleon for his own use. Right from the start the ideals of the revolution are being betrayed from within.

CHAPTER THREE

In the fervour of idealism all the animals work extremely hard. The clever pigs discover various ways for them to use the farm machinery without their having to stand on two legs and so imitate the humans. Note that the pigs themselves carefully avoid doing any manual labour. They direct the work while the rest of the creatures obey them. Because of their enthusiasm, the animals gather in the biggest harvest the farm has ever known. Because the food is theirs and they have worked so hard for it, every mouthful is a delight.

The animals, none the less, encounter a number of technical problems. They have no threshing machine, for example, but the pigs work out a way round this. The enormous strength of Boxer is absolutely essential to the farm's success. Orwell presents Boxer as a whole-hearted but simple idealist. He works like three horses. He is always seen where the work is hardest. He gets up half an hour earlier than anyone else. When things go wrong he has his own personal motto to encourage him: 'I will work harder!'

Though life on the farm is hard, it is in many ways ideal. However, not all the animals are truly at one with the revolutionary fervour. Mollie has a way of avoiding hard work. So, too, has the cat. Benjamin seems quite unchanged, too. He works as hard as he must, though never harder. He expresses no opinions about the rebellion, merely saying that he has lived a long time and seen many things.

At first, Sunday is a day off. After breakfast comes the farm meeting and the raising of the flag. Just as the Russian communists adopted as their symbol the red flag decorated with the hammer of industrial work and the sickle of agricultural labour, so the animals on the farm have a green flag (green being the colour of the fields), which is adorned with a hoof and a horn. These are symbolic of the farm animals across the world who will one day rise up and overthrow the human race.

After the raising of the flag the meeting begins. Needless to say, the pigs are wholly in charge. They put forward all the new resolutions, all the new ideas that they think the farm should adopt. The other animals understand how to vote on these resolutions, but they can never think of any resolutions of their own to put forward.

But the pigs are divided amongst themselves. In particular Snowball and Napoleon are rarely in agreement. It seems as if they actively search for issues to row over. This does not promise well, but for the moment the meetings end in harmony as all the animals sing 'Beasts of England'.

Snowball in particular is keen to advance the cause of the revolution. Just as the intellectual Trotsky set up innumerable plans to help improve the lives of the Russian people, so Snowball sets up committees to increase production, improve health and further the cause of education. None of these projects is successful, however, with the exception of the reading and writing classes.

We have seen that the pigs can read and write fluently. The dogs also learn to read fairly well, but they are only interested in reading the Seven Commandments. In other words, they use their skills not to broaden their minds but to make firm their sympathy with the revolution. This suggests the dogs are narrow and bigoted. It comes as no surprise that it is from among them that Napoleon's terrible personal police force will soon be recruited.

Clover and Boxer, representatives of the ordinary working people, have more difficulties with reading. Clover learns the alphabet but cannot string words together. Poor Boxer is incapable of learning more than four letters at a time. The vain little Mollie is only interested in spelling out her own name. This ignorance and lack of intelligence will be exploited by the pigs.

The pigs rapidly take advantage of the other animals' stupidity. Many of them not only fail to learn to read but are unable even to memorize the Seven Commandments. Snowball has an answer to this. Rather than try to get the duller animals to think, he reduces the Seven Commandments to one simple slogan: 'Four legs good, two legs bad'. The sheep, who are the most stupid of all the animals, bleat this mindless slogan out all day long.

Napoleon, more devious than Snowball, scorns his rival's attempts to improve life on the farm. Besides, he has his own sinister purposes, his own view of how he can advance his personal power. The dogs give birth to puppies, and as soon as these are weaned, Napoleon quietly takes them from their mothers and secretly educates them. A moment of suspicion perhaps flickers in our minds: what is Napoleon's purpose here? Orwell does not tell us yet. Instead he makes us focus on another of the pigs' deceits.

The apples are ripening in the orchard and the windfalls are already lying on the grass. In their simple, trusting way the animals think that these apples will be shared equally between them. Not a bit of it. The windfalls are to be gathered for the use of the pigs alone. Some of the other animals begin to complain about this. The pigs send out their propaganda agent to quieten them down.

Notice the creepy way in which Squealer justifies his masters' decision. It was said earlier that Squealer could turn black into white. Now we see him in action. He says he hopes that the animals do not think the pigs are being selfish. Many of them actually dislike apples. He does not like them himself. The only reason that the pigs want the apples is to preserve their health. They have already commandeered the milk supplies, and now Squealer tells the animals that 'Science' has shown that these nutritious foods are absolutely essential to the well-being of brain-workers like the pigs. Squealer declares that a great burden of administration falls on the long-suffering pigs. If they relax their efforts, Jones will come back. Surely they would not want that, would they? Better to give the milk and apples to the pigs than suffer the indignity of Jones's return.

Squealer's is an excessively hypocritical speech, which shows how a clever manipulator of words can bamboozle people into accepting any injustice. This is propaganda in action, and it is the means by which the animals are persuaded to accept the slow collapse of their rebellion from idealism to tyranny. There are no complaints when the pigs order that the main crop of apples should be theirs as well.

CHAPTER FOUR

News of the rebellion has spread. Just as the Russian Bolsheviks sent out agents to tell of the success of their revolution, so Snowball and Napoleon have sent out flights of pigeons to tell the neighbouring farms about their achievements.

Mr Jones, meanwhile, is spending his time at the Red Lion, bemoaning his fate. The other farmers appear sympathetic but do little to help him. Indeed, they wonder if they can turn his bad luck to their advantage. Two of Mr Jones's fellow farmers figure in particular. The first of these is Mr Pilkington, an easy-going, old-fashioned gentleman farmer, who is the owner of Foxwood. In the allegory he represents Winston Churchill. The other farmer is Mr Frederick. He is a hard man, always involved in lawsuits. His farm is called Pinchfield. In the allegory Mr Frederick represents Hitler.

Orwell makes it clear that Mr Pilkington and Mr Frederick dislike each other in just the way that Churchill and Hitler were enemies. Both Pilkington and Frederick are worried by the animals' rebellion, however. Similarly both Churchill and Hitler were concerned about the rise of Russian communism. For a while the farmers try to laugh the rebellion off. They also start spreading rumours. First they pretend that the animals are divided among themselves and are starving to death. When it becomes clear that this is not so, they start spreading rumours about life on the farm. They talk of cannibalism, torture and immorality.

No one really believes these stories, and animals on other farms become restless when they hear of the rebellion. Across the length and breadth of the country animals start singing 'Beasts of England' and are punished for it.

After the October harvest a flight of pigeons descends on Animal Farm and tells the occupants that Jones and his allies are preparing to attack. In terms of the allegory this represents the forces of the counter-revolution and their opposition to Soviet communism.

Notice that it is Snowball who takes the initiative here. It is he who plans the animals' defence strategies and it is he who leads them. Napoleon appears to take no part in the campaign. None the less, it will be part of Napoleon's tactics in his rise to power to present

Snowball's activities as those of a traitor. Thus will propaganda and lies corrupt the truth and lead to tryanny.

Snowball's military campaign has been carefully prepared. First comes a light skirmishing manoeuvre and then a strong attack. The humans manage to beat this off, but then, at a signal from Snowball, the animals retreat. The men rush triumphantly into the yard and are immediately surrounded by an ambush. Snowball gives the order to advance, rushes at Jones and sustains a number of wounds. One of the sheep is killed. Boxer, meanwhile, rears up on his hind legs and thrashes out with his great hooves. His strength is truly terrifying and he appears to kill a stable-lad from Foxwood. At this the men panic and run away. The animals chase them from the farm with great vigour.

Boxer is deeply upset by the thought that he has killed the stable-boy. Snowball tells him not to be sentimental and adds that the only good human is a dead one. It turns out that the stable-boy has, in fact, only been knocked unconscious.

It is then noticed that Mollie is missing. It is feared that she has been abducted, but she has hidden herself in her stall, frightened by the battle.

The triumphant animals now celebrate their victory. They sing 'Beasts of England' and give the dead sheep a solemn funeral. Snowball makes a speech, and he and Boxer are each awarded a medal for their bravery. The dead sheep, too, is given a posthumous award. It is agreed that the victory over Jones shall be called the Battle of the Cowshed. Mr Jones's gun, which was knocked from his hands, is placed in triumph by the flagstaff, and it is decreed that it will be fired twice a year – once to celebrate the anniversary of the Battle of the Cowshed and once on Midsummer's Day to celebrate the anniversary of the rebellion itself.

CHAPTER FIVE

This chapter presents one of the great turning-points in the novel. It shows how the animals' rebellion and all their high ideals are betrayed by Napoleon as he becomes a tyrant.

First of all we are shown Mollie's defection. We are told that she has not been working as hard as she should. She is then confronted by Clover, who tells her that she thinks she has seen Mollie talking to one of Mr Pilkington's men and allowing him to stroke her nose. In other words, the White Russians are beginning to make overtures to the Western capitalists. Mollie strongly but unconvincingly denies this and gallops away. However, when Clover goes to inspect her stall, she finds sugar lumps and bunches of ribbons hidden there. Three days later Mollie disappears. It is eventually discovered that she has gone over to the human beings and is working for a man who dresses her up prettily and harnesses her to his dogcart. In her own way Mollie has betrayed the rebellion. She is never mentioned again.

Cold winter comes to Animal Farm. The meetings in the barn become more acrimonious. Snowball and Napoleon disagree on everything and there are violent debates. Snowball usually wins the majority vote, but Napoleon is more successful in establishing his influence at other times. In particular he has trained the sheep to bleat out their slogan 'Four legs good, two legs bad' whenever Snowball's speeches seem to be winning the day. Snowball is still enthusiastic about schemes for improvement, but Napoleon says these will come to nothing.

Their most bitter wrangle is about the building of the windmill. In terms of the allegory this represents a major issue in the Russian Revolution. Trotsky was convinced that Russia needed to modernize her methods of industrial production. Factories would have to be built and efficiency introduced. Stalin, on the other hand, was more concerned to rationalize agricultural production, and he set about 'collectivizing' the farms. This meant that the peasants themselves no longer ran the farms but were obliged to surrender them to state control.

Snowball has decided that the windmill should be built on the highest hill on the farm. He has great schemes for improvement, which the windmill will bring about. It will operate a dynamo, provide electricity, warm the animals in winter and run their machines. The animals are amazed by these dreams of modernization.

Snowball works very hard at his plans. He spends hours in a shed, making drawings and calculations. All the animals regard this as wonderful, even through they do not really understand what the drawings mean. Only Napoleon professes to despise Snowball's efforts. One day he walks into the shed, looks contemptuously at the plans, urinates on them and leaves.

The issue of the windmill becomes a major topic of conversation. Snowball does not deny how difficult it will be to build, but maintains that it can be completed within a year. The animals will then be able to enjoy a three-day week. Napoleon declares that the whole scheme is a waste of time and that the animals will starve to death if they give all their energies to building it. At the meetings some side with Snowball, others with Napoleon. Benjamin refuses to support either party. The cynical old donkey does not believe that life will ever be substantially improved.

A second issue also divides the animals, one which again parallels a crucial argument among the Bolsheviks. This issue concerns the defence of the farm and the future of Animalism. Like Trotsky, Snowball believes that if the animals on all the neighbouring farms are converted to Animalism, then they will have no enemies and so will not need to defend themselves. Napoleon strongly disagrees with this. Like Stalin, he believes that Animal Farm should stockpile weapons and train for war. The rest of the animals cannot make up their minds about this.

Matters come to a head at a Sunday Meeting. We have seen that these meetings have so far been run with at least an appearance of democracy. The animals have been allowed to vote on the various proposals put to them. Napoleon, however, has long realized that this is no way to effectively establish his personal power. At the meeting he quietly opposes plans for building the windmill and then sits down. Snowball makes a passionate speech in praise of the windmill and the benefits it will bring. The animals are completely carried away by his vision of an ideal future.

The time has now come for Napoleon to assert his power. He throws a strange look at Snowball and utters a peculiar, high-pitched whimper. The puppies that Napoleon took from their mothers and trained then come rushing in. By now fully grown, they make a terrible baying sound and are wearing hideous brass-studded collars. Just as Stalin maintained his power through the strength of his terrible secret police force, so Napoleon has his own private army. The dogs make straight for Snowball and chase him across the farm. He only just escapes them as he slips through the hedges. He is never seen again.

The animals are terrified by this turn of events. But it is only the first of the horrors that will be inflicted on them now that Napoleon has established absolute power. Surrounded by his dogs he stands where old Major had once delivered his idealistic speech outlining the principles of Animalism. These principles will now be destroyed one by one. Napoleon declares that voting will no longer take place at the Sunday Meetings. For him democracy is simply a waste of time. Just as Stalin made sure that all decisions were the work of the Politburo, so Napoleon makes sure that all decisions on Animal Farm are made by an inner committee of the pigs. All that the rest of the animals will have to do is to hoist their flag, sing 'Beasts of England' and obey.

Even Boxer is vaguely troubled by this, while some of the young pigs loudly express their disapproaval. Napoleon's dogs immediately threaten them and they fall silent. The sheep, meanwhile, bleat out their mindless slogan.

Orwell shows how tyranny is supported by violence, injustice and sheer stupidity. He shows also that tyranny needs a propaganda machine. Squealer is sent round the farm to explain Napoleon's actions. He tells them of the gruelling burden of work that Napoleon now has to shoulder. He tells them also that where they might make the wrong decisions, the idealistic Napoleon will always be right. For example, the animals might have agreed to the building of the windmill. This idea was a ridiculous one, and Snowball himself is no better than a criminal. Propaganda is beginning to twist the truth.

One of the animals mentions how bravely Snowball fought at the Battle of the Cowshed. Squealer declares that bravery is not enough and that Snowball's part in the battle has probably been exaggerated. Discipline is what is needed. Without discipline Jones might well return. None of the animals would want that, would they? Once again this argument appears unanswerable.

Orwell shows that the stupid but loyal Boxer is the victim of wicked propaganda. Boxer completely denies himself the right to any opinion. For him 'Napoleon is always right'. In such ways do simple people deny themselves political power. This is a bleak and terrible comment.

Spring returns to the farm, and at the Sunday Meetings orders for the week are given out. The flag is raised and the animals are required to troop past the skull of old Major in reverence. Napoleon, Squealer and a pig called Minimus (in the allegory Minimus represents the Russian poet Mayakovsky) sit on a platform apart from the rest of the animals, surrounded by the dogs. Napoleon has become the complete dictator of the farm.

We now see Napoleon's absolute power in action. Three weeks after Snowball's expulsion Napoleon declares that the windmill will be built after all. He gives no reason for this change of mind, but merely declares that it will mean very hard work and even a reduction in rations. In terms of the allegory Napoleon's decision to build the windmill is an exact parallel to Stalin's first Five-Year Plan for the modernization of Russia. Just as this resulted in terrible suffering for the Russian people and eventually proved a failure, so Napoleon's decision to build the windmill will cause great hardship and will seem to end in disaster.

The tyrant again needs his propaganda machine to explain his decision to the people. Squealer declares that Napoleon was never really opposed to the windmill; indeed, it was his idea all along. Snowball had, in fact, stolen the plans from him. This, of course, is nonsense, and one of the animals asks why Napoleon had spoken against the scheme if it was originally his idea. Squealer looks very sly. He has to summon up all his devious abilities if he is to explain this awkward problem away.

He says that Napoleon only *seemed* to oppose the scheme. It was a cunning manoeuvre to get rid of Snowball, who was in fact a very dangerous character. Such behaviour is called 'tactics'. The animals are not quite sure that they understand this, but Squealer talks so persuasively and the dogs that surround him seem so fierce that no more questions are asked. Opposition has been silenced. Absolute tyranny is supported by lies and threats. Animal Farm has become a police state.

CHAPTER SIX

The animals work like slaves. They often put in a sixty-hour week. Napoleon declares that there will also be voluntary work on Sunday afternoons. Anybody not volunteering for this work will have his or her rations halved.

None the less, much important work on the farm does not get done, and it is clear that a hard winter is in store for the animals. The building of the windmill causes many problems. Stone, sand and cement are available, but it is only with great difficulty that the animals manage to break the stones down into suitable sizes. This they do by dragging them up a hill and then dropping them over the edge so they break. All of this requires enormous physical effort, and Boxer's great physical strength is absolutely essential. Clover warns him not to overwork himself, but the simple, loyal cart-horse takes no notice and repeatedly mutters his two mottoes to himself. He vows that he will work harder. He tells himself that Napoleon is always right. His cockerel now wakes him three quarters of an hour earlier than the rest of the animals. He also works in his spare time.

Because Jones has gone, the animals have enough food to feed themselves. They also do such jobs as weeding better than the humans could. None the less, shortages occur. The animals also need a number of things the farm cannot produce for itself. The animals do not see how these problems can be solved.

Napoleon, of course, has an answer. This answer is yet another betrayal of the principles of Animalism. Old Major had declared that no animal should ever handle money or engage in trade. Napoleon now makes arrangements to sell a stack of hay and some of the animals' wheat. Also the hens are told that they may well have to sacrifice some of their eggs. In his speech at the start of the novel Major declared that the sale of eggs was one of the unnecessary cruelties inflicted by Jones on the animals. Notice how subtly Orwell presents Napoleon's change from revolutionary to capitalist.

The animals are made uneasy by Napoleon's decision, but are silenced by the growling of the dogs and the bleating of the sheep. Napoleon then declares that all the arrangements have been made and the animals themselves will not need to come into contact with human beings. Napoleon will arrange everything through his agent – Mr Whymper, the solicitor. The meeting ends with the singing of 'Beasts of England'.

Squealer is then sent round the farm to smooth over any problems. He tells the animals that the resolution against engaging in trade has never actually been passed. Indeed, he suggests that the whole idea is an illusion, a lie put about by Snowball. Certainly the resolution has never been written down, and so the animals must be mistaken.

Mr Whymper visits the farm every Monday. He is a sly little man, and the animals dread his appearance. None the less, they feel proud when they see Napoleon giving him orders. We are told that the humans (or capitalists) hate the very existence of the farm and devoutly hope that it will soon go bankrupt. Nevertheless they cannot help having a measure of respect for the animals'achievements. At last they even begin to call the place Animal Farm. They no longer believe that Jones will return.

For the moment Whymper is the only human being who has any contact with the animals, but rumours are circulating that Napoleon is about to enter into an agreement with either Mr Pilkington or Mr Frederick. In terms of the political allegory this represents the over-tures made by Stalin to both Churchill and Hitler. Just as Stalin's foreign policy resulted in the invasion of Russia and the suffering of her people, so Napoleon's attempts to negotiate with the two farmers will lead to invasion and great suffering for the animals.

Another principle of Animalism is now corrupted. The pigs move into the farmhouse. Squealer explains this away by saying that the pigs need somewhere quiet to work. He also shows us how Napoleon is becoming more and more obsessed with the glamour of his position. He is referred to as 'leader', and it is said that his new dignity requires a house to support it. Some of the animals believe that Napoleon is also sleeping in a bed.

Clover in particular is worried about this and goes with Muriel to consult the Seven Commandments. The Fourth Commandment had decreed that no animal should ever sleep in a bed. They now discover that the Fourth Commandment has been subtly changed. It declares that no animal shall sleep in a bed 'with sheets'. In such ways is truth perverted in a dictatorship. Propaganda works through lies and half-truths. Once again Squealer is able to convince the animals that all is well. Some days later he also has to persuade them that it is perfectly in order for the pigs to get up an hour later than everyone else.

The windmill is now half completed. This gives the animals great pleasure, and in what spare moments they have, they wander round it, admiring its apparent strength. Only the cynical Benjamin is un-impressed. One night, in the violent November winds, the windmill is blown down. The animals are plunged into despair. Even Napoleon seems to be lost for words.

But a tyrant can turn everything to his own advantage. Napoleon suddenly declares that the windmill has been wrecked not by the wind but by Snowball. He declares that Snowball has crept into the farm by night to destroy the animals' hard work. He pronounces the death penalty on his rival and rewards for anyone who brings him to justice. The animals believe Napoleon, and a great cry of indignation goes up. A pig's footprints are then discovered. They are believed to be Snowball's, and it is declared that they lead in the direction of Foxwood Farm. Napoleon unites the animals by getting them to hate Snowball. They begin at once on the rebuilding of the mill.

CHAPTER SEVEN

The animals rebuild the windmill during the bitter winter, well aware that they are being watched by the outside world. The humans know that the mill fell down because it was not strong enough. The animals, however, continue to believe Napoleon's propaganda and think that the calamity was all due to Snowball. They decide to build the mill twice as strong as before. This involves incredibly hard work, and only Boxer and Clover never lose heart.

By January food is running short and it is discovered that the potato crop has rotted in the frost. Starvation threatens. The humans spread rumours that the animals are dying of famine and disease, that they are fighting each other and even indulging in cannibalism and child murder.

Napoleon has to put a stop to this and uses Whymper for his purposes. Whymper is now shown carefully selected aspects of life on the farm. Napoleon also contrives that Whymper should see what appear to be full bins of grain. These have in fact been filled with sand on which a little wheat has then been scattered.

Just as Stalin's first Five-Year-Plan resulted in failure and great suffering, so do Napoleon's schemes on Animal Farm. Again, just as

Stalin became obsessed with his own glory, appearing only rarely and surrounded by pomp, so Napoleon becomes an increasingly remote figure. He issues his orders through Squealer, who informs the chickens that they must now surrender their eggs for sale.

The hens bitterly resent this, just as the Russian peasantry bitterly resented the collectivization of their farms. Indeed, just as the peasants did actual physical damage to their farms, so the hens smash their eggs rather than surrender them to Napoleon. The dogs are sent in, nine hens die and their deaths are falsely attributed to natural causes. The outside world knows nothing of all this. The eggs are delivered to market.

What we see here is the beginning of a reign of terror. Once Stalin became the supreme master of the Russian people, he too started a reign of terror. Millions of people were killed as he set about eliminating every form of opposition. Anybody who was in the least critical of him or who could be shown to be sympathetic to Trotsky was murdered. This is one of the most brutal periods in the history of the twentieth century, and for many years the Russian people were not allowed to know the full truth of what had happened.

Orwell creates a similar situation in *Animal Farm.* The imaginary treasons of Snowball become an obsession. Rumours abound. During the course of Chapter Seven these will lead to horrific events.

Again, just as Stalin indulged in a long series of devious negotiations with the West while organizing his reign of terror at home, so Napoleon now begins negotiations with Pilkington and Frederick over the sale of a pile of timber. Napoleon hesitates between the two, and whenever he appears to be about to settle with one of the farmers, rumours are put about that Snowball is sheltering on the other's farm.

It is then said that Snowball is coming to Animal Farm at night and causing havoc. Though it is obvious to the reader that this is not true, all the animals believe it. Fear of Snowball becomes hysterical, and Napoleon exploits this with all his evil genius. Just as Stalin brought thousands of innocent people before his dreadful courts, made them confess to all sorts of crimes they had never committed and then had them executed, so Napoleon does the same with the animals on the farm. Stalin's purges are re-created in all their terrifying cruelty.

Squealer is essential to Napoleon's purposes here. He whips up hatred of Snowball to fever pitch and tells many lies in the process. He even declares that Snowball was working for Mr Jones. Squealer claims he has documents to prove this. He then goes on to say that Snowball was working for the defeat of the animals at the Battle of the Cowshed. This is patently absurd. The animals can barely believe what they are hearing. Even Boxer, slow-witted though he is, is moved to ask some awkward questions. Once again Squealer manages to argue that black is white. He says that if only Boxer were able to read, he would see that the documents Squealer has unearthed would prove everything. However, since Boxer is unable to read, he has to take Squealer's word that it was Napoleon and not Snowball who saved the day at the Battle of the Cowshed. In fact, of course, Orwell very carefully described Snowball's bravery in the conflict and did not mention Napoleon's part in it at all.

Squealer's description of the battle is so vivid that the animals are almost convinced. When Squealer then says that Napoleon has stated 'categorically' that Snowball was Jones's agent, Boxer is prepared to believe him, reasoning that 'Napoleon is always right'.

The terrible purges now begin. A meeting is held in the yard. Napoleon emerges, adorned with the medals he has awarded himself and surrounded by his dogs. The animals realize that something terrible is about to happen.

Napoleon utters his awful cry, his dogs leap forward, seize four pigs by the ears and drag them, bleeding, to their master's feet. Maddened by the taste of blood, three of the dogs then leap on Boxer, who easily fends them off. One of the dogs is pinned to the ground by Boxer's hoof, and the cart-horse looks at his master, wondering whether he should kill it. Napoleon sharply orders him to let it go.

The wounded pigs now confess to their crimes. They are the pigs who originally protested against the abolition of voting at the Sunday Meetings. In quivering terror they admit they are in contact with Snowball, and collaborated with him in destroying the windmill, and that they plotted to hand the farm over to Mr Frederick. They also admit that Snowball was Jones's agent. When their confessions are complete, the dogs leap on them and tear their throats out.

The three hens who led the rebellion over the eggs also confess and are slaughtered. A goose and three sheep also die. The Sixth

Commandment of Animalism has been broken: animals have killed each other. The air is heavy with the smell of blood.

Such terror makes the animals miserable. Since the expulsion of Jones, no animal had killed another. Now mass murders are taking place. Boxer grieves but cannot understand what is going on. He believes that in some vague way the troubles are his fault. The only solution he can see is to work harder. He vows to get up an hour earlier every morning. He then lumbers off to collect stones for the windmill.

The rest of the animals huddle silently round Clover. The farm looks beautiful in the light of the spring evening. Clover is moved to tears as she contrasts the beauty and the high hopes she once had with the reality of the slaughter that is taking place on the farm. She realizes that the principles of Animalism have been destroyed. Fear has taken the place of freedom, but she does not wish to rebel. She believes that even under Napoleon's reign of terror the animals are better off than they were under Mr Jones. She will continue to work hard and be loyal, despite her sadness.

To cheer up her spirits Clover begins to sing 'Beasts of England'. The other animals join in. As they finish the song for the third time, Squealer appears. He tells them that 'Beasts of England' is now forbidden. It was the battle-cry of the rebellion, but the rebellion is now over. He declares that the better world the song promised has come about. The sheep drown all opposition with their mindless bleating. 'Beasts of England' is replaced by a poor substitute and is never heard again. The revolution has been betrayed once more.

CHAPTER EIGHT

When the terror caused by the trials and the murders begins to pass, some of the animals remember how the Sixth Commandment forbade any form of slaughter. Clover asks Benjamin to take her to read the commandments painted on the barn wall, but he refuses, saying that it is not for him to meddle in the affairs of the farm. Clover eventually persuades Muriel to accompany her, and we discover that yet another of the commandments has been subtly changed. It is now decreed that no animal shall kill another 'without cause'. Clover seems to think that the command has always been thus. As a result she believes that the killings are justified. We, who know what has happened, see Clover as the pathetic dupe of Napoleon's deceit.

The animals work extremely hard on the rebuilding of the windmill. Sometimes it seems to them that life is more demanding than it was under Jones. It also seems to them sometimes that they are not so well fed. Squealer produces reams of statistics to prove that this is not so. Though the animals see no reason to disbelieve him, we guess that these statistics are forgeries.

Meanwhile Napoleon is retreating into increasingly splendid isolation. A black cockerel precedes his rare appearances, while it is said that he lives in separate apartments in the farmhouse and eats off a Crown Derby dinner serivce. It is also decreed that his birthday shall be celebrated by the firing of Mr Jones's gun. Napoleon is constantly referred to now by a series of ludicrous titles. Squealer's propaganda machine is working hard, and Napoleon acquires almost mythical status among the rest of the animals. Minimus composes an absurd hymn of praise to Napoleon, which is painted on the barn opposite the Seven Commandments with a portrait of Napoleon above it.

Napoleon is also continuing his complex negotiations with the outside world. These centre on selling a pile of timber to Frederick and Pilkington. In terms of the political allegory this represents Stalin's attempts to do business openly with England and secretly with Germany. None the less, rumours keep circulating that Frederick wishes to attack the farm and that Snowball is involved in this. Three hens confess to being confederates of Snowball's and plotting to murder Napoleon. They are immediately executed. A guard is put round Napoleon at night and a special dog tastes his food for poison.

It is now announced that Napoleon has decided to sell the timber to Pilkington. Negotiations are conducted through Whymper. The animals dislike Pilkington but are even more terrified of Frederick. It is now said that Frederick is about to invade the farm and has bribed the forces of justice to make sure that no questions are asked about his invasion. In addition to this, stories of Frederick's obscene cruelty to his animals abound. In terms of the allegory these stories represent the appalling suffering inflicted by Hitler on the Jews and other minority groups. Though Squealer tells the animals to trust Napoleon, feelings against Frederick run high. Napoleon then announces that he never intended to sell the timber to Frederick. He also sends out batches of pigeons to spread the slogan 'Death to Frederick'.

Further evidence of Snowball's apparent treachery is brought to light. Weeds in the wheat crop are said to be his doing, and a gander who is persuaded to admit to his part in the crime commits suicide by swallowing deadly nightshade berries. The animals are also informed that Snowball was never awarded a medal for bravery at the Battle of the Cowshed. Indeed, he was censured for cowardice in the fight. Yet again it takes all Squealer's powers of persuasion to convince the animals that their memories have played tricks on them.

At last the windmill is finished. Its completion is a triumph of sheer hard work, and the animals are very proud of themselves. They admire the thick walls especially. It seems that only explosives would ever bring them down. They gambol round the windmill in sheer joy. Napoleon congratulates them and announces that the mill will be called Napoleon Mill.

Two days later Napoleon announces another of his surprise decisions. He has sold the timber to Frederick. It is revealed that his apparent friendship with Pilkington was merely a device to raise the price of the timber. Napoleon assures the animals that Frederick does not intend an invasion. He adds that rumours of Frederick's cruelty have been greatly exaggerated. The pigs are delighted by Napoleon's cunning.

They are even more impressed when they are told that he has insisted on being paid in cash rather than with a cheque. Frederick has already handed over the £5 notes and is busy carting the timber away. Napoleon proudly displays the banknotes to the animals, but three days later they are informed of something terrible. The banknotes are forgeries. Napoleon has been wholly taken in by the cunning Frederick. In terms of the political allegory the phoney banknotes represent the phoney non-aggression treaty signed by Hitler and Stalin. Just as Frederick is about to invade Animal Farm, so Hitler invaded Eastern Europe almost immediately after signing his treaty with Stalin.

Napoleon vows revenge, but Frederick's attack takes place the following morning. Like Hitler's invasion of Russia, it is a large-scale operation. Although it is hideously destructive, it is eventually repelled. Frederick's men inflict terrible pain with their guns, and some of the animals are seriously wounded. The enemy also gets possession of the windmill. Napoleon is deeply worried and hopes that Pilkington will send him help, just as Stalin hoped that the Allies would help him against the fascists and Hitler. No such help is forthcoming. Pilkington merely sends a message saying 'Serve you right'. The animals are on their own, just as the Russians were.

Frederick and his men gather round the windmill, drill a hole in its base, load it with explosives and blow the windmill sky-high. The animals' labours lie in ruins, just as Russia's factories were destroyed in the German invasion. Rage gives the animals new courage and they fight with all the fury they can muster. In just the same way millions of Russians fought with supreme bravery at the Battle of Stalingrad and were eventually successful in driving Hitler back.

Frederick, too, is repulsed by the animal forces, who then limp back to the farm to bury their dead and mourn the destruction of the windmill. Rebuilding it a second time is going to be a terrible task. Though they have won the battle, the animals feel defeated by the destruction of their efforts and it takes all of Squealer's skill to give them new heart. We are told that Squealer himself has taken no part in the action.

Boxer has been wounded in the hoof. He realizes what a monumental task lies before him in the rebuilding of the windmill, and for the first time he feels old.

A victory celebration is held. The dead animals are buried. Napoleon walks at the head of the funeral procession. It is decreed that the encounter with Frederick shall be called the Battle of the Windmill. Napoleon awards himself the Order of the Green Banner.

Another of the Seven Commandments is now broken. The pigs discover a case of whisky, which they proceed to drink. A drunken party takes place in the farmhouse. Once it had been decreed that no animal should drink alcohol. Napoleon gets so drunk, however, that he even dresses up in Mr Jones's clothes. His progress towards a state of corruption equal to that of the humans he has replaced is made very clear. However, Napoleon has drunk so much of the whisky that the following morning he suffers from a dreadful hangover. The pigs think he is dying. This causes great dismay and it is rumoured that

Snowball has poisoned him. Napoleon recovers, however and decrees that the drinking of alcohol shall be punished by death. The following day he instructs Whymper to go to Willingdon and buy some books on home brewing. The paddock, which had once been put aside for retired animals, is ploughed up and sown with barley. Clearly Napoleon intends brewing his own alcohol.

Squealer then goes out at midnight to make further subtle changes to the Seven Commandments. He falls off his ladder but is protected by the dogs, who escort him back to the farmhouse. Only the cynical Benjamin realizes what has happened. He says nothing, but a few days later Muriel discovers that the Fifth Commandment is no longer quite what she remembers it to have been. It now reads: 'No animal shall drink alcohol *to excess.*'

CHAPTER NINE

Despite the fact that his hoof takes a long time to heal, Boxer does not take so much as a day off work. Clover treats the hoof with poultices, while Boxer himself declares that his only ambition now is to see the completion of the windmill before he retires. There is much talk about the generous arrangements made for the animals' retirement, but these are merely talk. The area where the retired animals were to live has been given over to Napoleon's barley.

Life continues to be hard and rations are short. Only the pigs and the dogs do not have their rations reduced. Once again Squealer has to persuade the animals that all is really well. Lists of phoney statistics convince the animals that everything is better than it was in Jones's time. In fact, most of the animals have forgotten what life was like in Jones's time. They are keenly aware, however, that they are now often hungry, cold and overworked. None the less, it gives them great comfort to think that they are free.

The following autumn Napoleon's wives produce thirty-one young pigs. Bricks and timber are purchased to build them a school. Napoleon teaches them himself. He declares that the other animals must stand aside when a pig approaches them. Also the pigs are allowed to wear green ribbons on their tails on Sundays.

Money remains a problem on the farm. Napoleon organizes more business deals, selling off hay, potatoes and eggs. Rations are reduced and lanterns in the stalls are forbidden. The pigs, meanwhile, continue to lead a life of comparative luxury. They have mastered the arts of brewing, and when the animals smell the delicious odour of cooking barley, they believe a special mash is being prepared for them. This is not so. All the barley is reserved for the pigs, who receive a pint of beer a day. Napoleon himself drinks four pints a day from the Crown Derby soup tureen.

The pigs try to offset the hardness of the other animals' lives with songs, speeches, processions and a weekly Spontaneous Demonstration. All of these are designed to make Napoleon appear even more glorious. The sheep bleat out their slogan to drown the opposition. All of these public ceremonies are part of a plan to make the animals forget they are hungry.

In April Napoleon is elected President of the Republic. He is the only candidate in the election. Further vilification of Snowball takes place, but in the summer a really surprising event occurs: Moses the raven returns. In terms of the political allegory this represents the meetings held between Stalin and a minor Roman Catholic official when Stalin was hoping to gain the support of the Papacy for his ruthless conduct in Catholic Poland. This came to nothing and the world laughed at Stalin for his foolishness.

Moses himself is quite unchanged. He still talks about the delights of Sugarcandy Mountain and even claims to have visited it. The pigs do not believe anything Moses says, yet they tolerate his presence. Some of the other animals, however, begin to believe his stories.

Boxer's wound heals and he works harder than ever. None the less, he is looking older. By springtime he is faltering in his work. He vows to work harder but is failing all the time. He is nearly twelve years old and is looking forward to his pension.

One summer evening Boxer falls and is unable to get up again. He is discovered with a thin trickle of blood running from his mouth. One of his lungs has given up, and he realizes that he must retire. The other animals run to fetch Squealer, while Clover and Benjamin remain beside Boxer. A quarter of an hour later Squealer reappears, declaring that Napoleon has made arrangments for Boxer to be sent to hospital in Willingdon. The animals are a little wary of this, but Squealer convinces them of Napoleon's noble intentions. Boxer is then taken back to his stall. He lies there for two days, dreaming of a happy retirement. Perhaps now he will even find time to learn to read.

Because of the amount there is to do on the farm, Benjamin and Clover can be with Boxer only when they have finished work, and it is during the middle of the day that a van comes for Boxer. Benjamin spots it and comes galloping over to tell the other animals what has happened. They rush back to the farm buildings and see that Boxer has already been loaded on to the van, which is driven by an exceptionally unpleasant-looking character.

The animals crowd round the van, wishing Boxer goodbye. Only the cynical but realistic Benjamin sees what is really happening. He alone has bothered to read the lettering painted on its side. This is no ambulance. It is the van of the horse slaughterer, who is taking Boxer to his death. The animals are horrified, but the van moves out of the yard before they can do anything.

Clover calls out pathetically, and as she does so, Boxer's stupid but kindly face appears at the little window at the back of the van. She begs him to try to escape. The other animals echo her cry, but the van is already speeding up and it is uncertain that Boxer knows what is going on. When he tries to escape, he finds that he is no longer strong enough. Though he beats at the side of the van, the sound of drumming hooves grows fainter and dies away as the van disappears. Though the animals beg the horses who are drawing the van to stop, they merely quicken their pace. Boxer is never seen again.

Three days later the animals are told that Boxer has died. Squealer gives a revoltingly hypocritical account of his last hours. As he finishes this, his eyes narrow with suspicion. He says that he has heard it rumoured that some of the animals think that Boxer has been taken to the knacker's yard. This is ridiculous. Napoleon would never allow such a thing. The van truly belonged to a vet who simply had not had the time to paint out the old inscription. The animals appear to believe this and are glad for the kindness they believe Napoleon has shown to Boxer.

Napoleon gives a short speech in Boxer's honour at the Sunday Meeting, and says that unfortunately it has not been possible to bring back Boxer's body. None the less a large wreath has been sent and the pigs are due to hold a memorial banquet in Boxer's honour. To end his hypocritical address Napoleon repeats Boxer's two favourite mottoes and tells the other animals they would do well to adopt them for themselves.

The final obscenity then takes place. We discover that the money the pigs have raised from selling Boxer to the knacker's yard has been spent on a crate of whisky. Another riotous party takes place in the farmhouse.

CHAPTER TEN

Several years have now passed since this degrading incident and many of the animals have died. We are told also that Jones is dead. Only Clover, Benjamin, Moses and a number of pigs remain from the old days. Many younger animals have been born, including a number of horses who remain as ill-educated as Boxer was. It is very doubtful if these horses really understand the nature of the rebellion. What Orwell is saying in terms of the political allegory is that it is very doubtful whether the great mass of the Russian people really understand the true nature of communism.

The farm is fairly prosperous now. It is also better organized and larger, two fields having been bought from Mr Pilkington. The windmill has been built yet again and various technological improvements have occured. None of these is used to the benefit of the animals. The windmill is employed to grind corn, which is then sold at a profit. The luxuries Snowball once promised are no longer even mentioned. Napoleon says they are decadent. True happiness, he declares, lies in hard work and frugal living.

Only the pigs and dogs appear to have benefited from any improvements made on the farm, and much of Squealer's propaganda is now given over to justifying the enormous amount of paperwork the pigs do, which is, he says, essential. We can guess that most of this work is mere bureaucratic nonsense. The other animals' lives continue to be as hard as ever, which, as Benjamin declares, is the unalterable way of things.

None the less the animals do not give up hope. They are proud to be the only farm in England run by its own animals. They are all intensely patriotic. The old dreams survive. The idealism in Major's speech has not been extinguished. Sometime soon the golden day of freedom will come. They still believe that all animals are equal.

Squealer now orders the sheep to follow him to an obscure part of the farm, where he busies himself teaching them. At night he returns to the farmhouse while the sheep stay on the waste ground. It emerges that he is teaching them a new song.

Then something appalling happens: Clover sees Squealer walking on two legs. The first and most basic principle of Animalism has been overthrown. Soon the animals see all the other pigs walking on their hind legs. Finally Napoleon emerges walking on two legs and carrying a whip in his trotter. The animals are reduced to silence by this absolute betrayal. In spite of the dogs the animals are about to protest, when the sheep bleat out the new and hypocritical slogan that Squealer has been busy teaching them: 'Four legs good, two legs *better*!' Protected by this outburst the pigs return to the farmhouse.

Clover, her eyes old and dim, nudges at Benjamin and leads him round to the barn where the Seven Commandments had once been written. Each of these has been betrayed. Now they have even been obliterated from the barn wall. Instead of the Seven Commandments there is only one meaningless, tyrannical and dreadful phrase:

**ALL ANIMALS ARE EQUAL
BUT SOME ANIMALS ARE MORE
EQUAL THAN OTHERS**

The high ideals of the revolution have been utterly betrayed. All the pigs now carry whips and become more and more like the loathed human beings. They buy a radio, install a telephone and take out subscriptions to cheap newspapers and magazines. Napoleon smokes a pipe. He even starts to wear Mr Jones's clothes, while his favourite sow dresses up in the finery once belonging to Mrs Jones. The revolution is hastening to its bitterly ironic end.

About a week later the neighbouring farmers are invited on a tour of inspection. They express admiration for what they see and are then invited to a party at the farmhouse. The other animals creep up to the windows to see what is happening. The faithful Clover leads the way. They see Napoleon seated at the head of the table, drinking a toast to the humans after playing a game of cards with them.

Mr Pilkington gives a pompous reply to Napoleon's speech. He declares that he is glad the old enmities have been set aside and that all the misunderstandings in the past have been cleared up. It is true the humans had been suspicious at first, but what they have seen today has convinced them that Animal Farm is a model of orderly discipline. Indeed, he approves of the fact that the lower animals work harder and are 'paid' less than workers on any farm anywhere else. That the pigs should receive such praise from their former capitalist enemies is appalling.

Pilkington rounds off his speech by declaring that there are no differences of interest between the pigs and the humans. They all face the same problems. Just as the pigs have a lower order of animals to cope with, so capitalist human beings have the lower classes to contend with. This offensive joke causes much laughter, and Pilkington ends his speech toasting the prosperity of Animal Farm.

Napoleon now declares he has a few words to say. He says he does not want to spread the revolution to other farms. He wants to live at peace with his neighbours. He tells Pilkington that legally the farm is the property of the pigs. Further, animals will be forbidden to call each other 'comrade'. They will also be forbidden to march past Major's skull in tribute. The hoof and horn have been removed from the green flag. Finally and most dreadfully of all Napoleon utters the ultimate hypocrisy: the farm will no longer be called Animal Farm but will revert to its old title of Manor Farm. It is as if the rebellion, all the high hopes, all the hard work and all the suffering have been for nothing. The absolute tyranny of Jones has been replaced by the absolute tyranny of the pigs. The revolution that started with promises of heaven on earth has been revealed as a complete 'swindle'. The dream has become a nightmare.

And it is with a nightmare vision that the novel concludes. The rest of the animals have crept away, but they return when they hear uproar in the farmhouse. A quarrel has broken out between the pigs and the humans over cheating at a game of cards. In terms of the allegory this represents the outbreak of the Cold War between Russia and the Western powers. As the other animals look on appalled, a subtle change comes over the faces of all in the room. It seems that the human beings and the pigs have become so alike in appearance that it is almost impossible to distinguish between them. Hope for a better world is finally and completely extinguished.

Characters

MAJOR

Old Major is the pig who represents Marx and Lenin in the novel. Marx and Lenin were respectively the inspirer and leader of the communist revolution in Russia. We are told that Major is twelve years old, that he has had over 400 children, that he has a stout, rather regal appearance and that he is wise and kindly. None the less, his tusks have never been cut and this perhaps suggests that there is still something fierce about him, something capable of attack.

Major is essentially a thinker. At the beginning of the novel we are told he has had a dream and that the rest of the farm animals – who clearly regard him with respect – want to hear about it. Major's speech to the assembled animals consists of an exposition of the basic ideals of communism. Major vividly describes the animals' unhappy lives, the reasons for their unhappiness, the remedies they should take and the vices they should look out for. He also teaches them 'Beasts of England' – the battle hymn of their revolution.

Major dies three days after his talk. His ideas are developed by the rest of the pigs and are then successively betrayed by them.

NAPOLEON

Napoleon comes to dominate the novel. He takes his name from the French emperor who started as a revolutionary and ended as a tyrant. In terms of the political allegory underlying *Animal Farm* Napoleon represents Stalin, the Russian leader who betrayed the communist revolution, setting up in place of liberty and justice the tyranny of a one-man state. In the figure of Napoleon, Orwell shows how all revolutions, although they start by offering heaven on earth, are betrayed from within until they bring about a nightmare of repression.

We are told that the pigs are the most intelligent animals on the farm and that they have codified the principles of Animalism in a form that the others can easily understand. They have also set about teaching and organizing the rest of the animals.

Napoleon's character begins to emerge in Chapter Two, where he is at first compared and contrasted to Snowball, the pig who represents Stalin's rival, Trotsky. We are told that Napoleon is a Berkshire boar and that he is the only one of this breed on the farm. This already suggests his unique nature. We are also told that he is large and fierce, not much of a talker, but a pig capable of getting his own way.

Throughout most of Chapter Two Napoleon seems to take second place to Snowball, who, we are told, is a far more articulate pig. None the less, Napoleon emerges in his true colours right at the end of the chapter. It is he who craftily arranges that the milk supplies should be for the use of the pigs only.

Orwell was keen to point out the importance of this deception. It is the first example of the dishonesty and crafty self-seeking by which the pigs – and Napoleon in particular – turn the ideals of the revolution to their own advantage. From the very start the pigs have decided that they will be the figures in power. They will seize all the advantages that the new way of life on the farm offers them.

In Chapter Three we learn of the constant disagreements between Napoleon and Snowball, but once again it is Snowball who seems to have the dominant place in our imaginations. He is full of ideas for improving life. These ideas Napoleon despises.

However, at the end of the chapter Napoleon's devious nature again emerges. First we are told that the dogs have had puppies. As soon as these puppies have been weaned, Napoleon takes them from their mothers and educates them in secret. The other animals soon forget about their existence. This episode is clearly designed to trigger suspicion in our minds, but Orwell very skilfully focuses our attention on yet another of the pigs' deceptions: the way in which they insist that all the apples should be theirs exclusively. To ensure this they use the skills of Squealer, their propaganda agent. Political deception is thus paired with the lies of propaganda. For the moment – and like the other animals on the farm – we forget all about Napoleon's dogs and the secret training he is giving them.

In Chapter Four we are shown the forces of the counter-revolution attacking the farm. Once again it is Snowball who seems to take pride of place. Indeed, Napoleon is not mentioned. None the less, when he achieves full personal power, it will be one of his first tasks to rewrite the history of the Battle of the Cowshed, playing down Snowball's part and suggesting his own glorious role. In such ways is the truth twisted in a tyranny.

Chapter Five is the turning-point in the novel. It is the chapter in which Napoleon fully emerges in his true colours. In terms of the political allegory underlying the work it is the chapter in which we see Stalin emerging as the dictator of Russia, just as Napoleon emerges as the dictator of Animal Farm.

The Sunday Meetings show how acrimonious the divisions between Napoleon and Snowball have become. They seem to disagree almost for the sake of disagreeing. Once again it is Snowball who emerges as the more brilliant talker, while Napoleon is more effective at gaining support outside the meetings. At the meetings themselves the sheep interrupt Snowball's flights of eloquence by bleating out their mindless slogan: 'Four legs good, two legs bad'.

Two issues in particular divide Snowball and Napoleon. These issues in turn suggest the pigs' respective attitudes to Animalism as well as highlighting the differences between the thinking of Stalin and the ideas held by Trotsky. Snowball supports both industrialization and the universal spread of communism. Hence his urging of the project to build the windmill and his belief that the animals should work to convert neighbouring farms to their beliefs rather than seeing them as potential enemies against whom defences must be prepared. In other words, we can see Snowball partly as an idealist.

Napoleon is far more cynical. He believes that the animals should prepare themselves against attack from enemy forces. He also believes that it is far more important that the farm's agriculture should be brought up to date than that the animals should concentrate on new industrial projects. Indeed, he believes – or appears to believe – that if the animals spend all their time on building the windmill, then they will not have enough food to last them through the winter.

The animals are deeply divided on these issues. So far they have always been used to discussing such matters at the Sunday Meetings and then voting on them. An appearance of democracy at least has been preserved on the farm. Now matters are to change radically. At the height of Snowball's speech in praise of the windmill, and when he seems to be carrying all before him, Napoleon's long-laid plans for power emerge in their true awfulness.

Napoleon lets out a curious high-pitched whimper and his trained dogs come rushing in, dressed in hideous spiked collars, and make straight for Snowball. What we see here is the equivalent of Stalin's secret police force in action. Democracy is no way for a dictator to emerge. Napoleon realizes this and so he destroys democracy. Fear takes the place of discussion. Snowball is chased from the farm and Napoleon takes absolute control. The Sunday Meetings are no longer a forum for democratic debate. All decisions will now be made by committees of the pigs. These correspond to the communist Politburo. Opposition is silenced by the dogs. Squealer, Napoleon's propaganda agent, skilfully smooths out any opposition to Napoleon's personal rule.

The end of Chapter Five shows how arbitrary Napoleon's decisions will be. He suddenly announces that the windmill will be built after all. It takes all of Squealer's propaganda skills to persuade the animals that this decision is the right one, and in this we see how a tyrant successfully secures his rule through the careful use of lies. In terms of the political allegory of *Animal Farm* the building of the windmill represents Stalin's first Five-Year-Plan for the modernization of the Russian economy. Just as this was a failure and caused the Russian people huge hardship and deprivation, so the building of the windmill will cause much suffering on Animal Farm.

It is under Napoleon's influence particularly that the Seven Commandments of Animalism are progressively twisted and betrayed to support Napoleon's tyranny. In Chapter Six he suddenly announces that the animals will engage in trade. He says this is necessary for the building of the windmill. Major's speech and the Seven Commandments had forbidden such activities and declared that the animals should never handle money. Napoleon silences all opposition, however, and declares that he has already employed a neighbouring solicitor – Mr Whymper – to conduct negotiations for them. The animals themselves will be protected from human influence.

Squealer once again manages to persuade the animals that Napoleon's decisions are for the best, just as he also manages to convince them of the necessity of the pigs' move into the farmhouse. He says that this is particularly necessary if the 'Leader' is to preserve his dignity. We see here that Napoleon is becoming increasingly obsessed by his own glory. This, along with the progressive corruption of the Seven Commandments, shows how the principles of Animalism are being destroyed and that all the animals are now very far from being equal.

Orwell has a particularly subtle way of showing this destruction of ideals. Each time one of the principles of Animalism is corrupted and one of the animals goes to read the commandments painted on the barn wall, they find that these have been secretly altered. For instance, it was once declared that no animal should sleep in a bed. It is now found that the commandment declares that no animal should sleep in a bed 'with sheets'. We know that Squealer is responsible for these small but lethal adjustments to the truth. The animals, however, mostly believe that they must have remembered the commandments wrongly. In their trusting naivety they are thus the dupes of propaganda.

Finally, at the end of Chapter Six, the windmill is blown down in a storm. This causes widespread despair and even Napoleon is temporarily lost for words. Then suddenly, with the evil genius of a tyrant who can turn anything to his own advantage, Napoleon declares that the windmill was not blown down by the storm at all but was wrecked by Snowball. Napoleon now makes sure that his great rival is seen as the enemy of the people. An epidemic of fear sweeps the farm.

By Chapter Seven the animals are near to starvation. Once again Napoleon resorts to various ruses to make sure that the outside world does not see the true state of affairs on the farm. None the less further measures have to be taken to improve the financial position of the farm, and Napoleon declares that the chickens will have to prepare themselves to sell their eggs, despite the fact that in his speech at the beginning of the book Major had declared that this was contrary to the true spirit of Animalism.

The chickens revolt at this, just as the Russian peasants preferred to destroy their crops rather than surrender to Stalin's plan for the collectivization of their farms. Napoleon sends in his dogs to crush their revolt. Another principle of Animalism has been destroyed – the animals are now killing each other.

Napoleon encourages the circulation of further rumours about his old rival, Snowball. Propaganda and lies about him are spread, while Napoleon becomes an increasingly remote figure, concerned only with his own importance. When he does finally emerge, it is to reveal the full terror of his absolute power. Just as in communist Russia Stalin began a series of terrible purges in which millions were murdered for opposing him or for being thought to have supported Trotsky, so now any animal on the farm who can be made to confess that he is in sympathy with Snowball is summarily executed. Life on the farm becomes one of deepening horror. The air is thick with the smell of blood. The rest of the animals become deeply depressed, and when they sing 'Beasts of England' to cheer their spirits, they are told that the old battle hymn of the revolution has been banned. Under Napoleon's rule, they are told, the glories promised by the song have come about. Nothing, of course, could be further from the truth.

Napoleon is becoming increasingly remote and autocratic and is obsessed with his own creature comforts. He encourages the most absurd flattery. He also engages in complex and devious negotiations with the outside world: with Mr Pilkington, who represents the British leader, and Frederick, who represents the German leader. Just as Stalin signed a phoney non-aggression pact with Hitler, who then invaded Eastern Europe, so Napoleon is tricked by Frederick into selling some timber in exchange for forged banknotes. Frederick then invades the farm, blows up the windmill and inflicts massive damage. The animals resist him with the utmost bravery, just as the Russians resisted Hitler with extraordinary heroism. Hitler was finally pushed back at the Battle of Stalingrad. Frederick is repulsed at the Battle of the Windmill.

Victory celebrations take place, but at the end of Chapter Eight we are shown yet another betrayal of the principles of Animalism. The pigs discover a crate of whisky and they learn to drink alcohol. Napoleon in particular drinks so much and wakes with such a terrible hangover that it is given out that he is dying. Of course he recovers, but he now takes a keen interest in brewing and has part of the farm set aside for growing barley from which his beer will be made. Once again one of the Seven Commandments is secretly altered. It had been declared in the old days that no animal should drink alcohol. It is now declared that no animal shall drink alcohol 'to excess'.

The cruelty of Napoleon becomes more terrible and more obvious. This is shown particularly in his treatment of Boxer. Boxer represents the ordinary working individuals who were originally to gain most from the revolution. Boxer has shown himself to be unfailingly loyal and hardworking throughout the entire novel. Now, when he collapses and is clearly about to die, Napoleon arranges that he should be sold to the knacker's yard. This is a hideous betrayal, and Orwell makes sure that he rouses our full measure of disgust. No betrayal of the ideals of Animalism is more repulsive and disgraceful than this one. The anger we feel is brought to its climax when we discover that the profits resulting from the sale of Boxer are spent on whisky.

The last chapter presents the final and complete betrayal of the animals' revolution. This is wholly the work of Napoleon. Years have passed and the farm is now comparatively prosperous. Any benefits this brings, however, go entirely to the pigs. We have already been told that Napoleon has fathered many children, and we may presume that these children will continue the exploitation started by their father.

The first dreadful sign of the final collapse of Animalism comes when the pigs are seen walking on their hind legs. At the start of the novel it was decreed that four legs were good and two legs were bad. Now, under the training of Squealer, the animals are made to believe that four legs are good but two legs are even better. Since Napoleon himself now no longer walks on his front legs, he can carry a whip in his trotter. He is becoming more and more like a man, more and more like a corrupt capitalist. He begins to wear human clothes, and he and the rest of the pigs buy a radio, subscribe to cheap newspapers and think of having a telephone installed.

The climax comes when Napoleon throws a party to which the neighbouring farmers are invited. This shows how Orwell believed that Stalin wholly compromised his position as the leader of a revolution when he met with Churchill and Roosevelt at the Tehran Conference, where, Orwell thought, the three men were plotting to divide the world between them.

Mr Pilkington gives a speech of praise of the farm and says he hopes that all differences between the human farms and Animal Farm have now been removed. Indeed they have. Under the rule of Napoleon Animal Farm has become as cruel and exploitative of the ordinary working animals as it was in the days of Jones.

When Napoleon replies to the toast, we see the full depths of his corruption. He says he does not want to spread the principles of Animalism. In other words, he no longer sees any need for the world-wide spread of the ideals of liberty and justice. He is going to stop the animals calling each other 'Comrade'. Equality is abolished. We have already heard that the lesser animals are exploited on Animal Farm as badly as they are on any human farm. Finally Napoleon declares that the name Animal Farm is to be used no more. The old name 'Manor Farm' will be used henceforth.

Nothing could show more powerfully the complete collapse of the principles of Animalism and the ideals outlined in old Major's speech. Napoleon is completely at one with the capitalists. He is as corrupt and exploitative as they are. Indeed, he now becomes at one with them. As the rest of the animals peer in through the farmhouse windows, we see Napoleon actually changing his appearance so that he resembles the humans.

None the less, relations between him and his new allies are not easy. Just as the Cold War broke out between communist Russia and the West, so, as humans and pigs cheat at a game of cards, we see suspicion breaking out between them.

So in spite of the new friendship between pigs and humans, the end of the novel is very bleak. We are shown how a revolution begun in idealism has been corrupted from within. It has been corrupted by Napoleon, who, in his pursuit of personal power, has brought such suffering to Animal Farm that it is as if the revolution has never taken place.

SNOWBALL

Snowball is Orwell's representation of Trotsky, Stalin's great rival. As with Napoleon we first see his personality emerging in Chapter Two. We are told that Snowball is a more lively pig than Napoleon.

He is also a faster talker and more inventive. None the less he is considered to be less deep a character.

Snowball throws himself into the animals' revolt with great energy and imagination, and in the early chapters he seems the more interesting of the two leading pigs. It is he who criticizes Mollie for her weaknesses and organizes the destruction of the cruel instruments with which Jones oppressed the animals before the revolution. We are told that Snowball is better at writing than Napoleon, and it is Snowball who paints out the name 'Manor Farm', replacing it with 'Animal Farm', and who paints the Seven Commandments on the barn wall and encourages the other animals to learn them by heart. Finally it is Snowball who first encourages all the animals to set to work in the fields at the end of the second chapter.

Despite this enthusiasm it is important that we do not see Snowball as a pure idealist. He is no such thing. Orwell himself was certain that Trotsky was as responsible for the Bolsheviks' takeover of the revolution as Stalin was. Similarly Snowball is as keen as Napoleon that the pigs should benefit most from the animals' revolution. For instance, he makes no objection to the pigs receiving the milk Napoleon steals for their use. Neither does he disapprove of them having all the apples from the fruit harvest.

None the less, he and Napoleon become increasingly opposed on almost every issue that arises. These differences of opinion become clearest at the Sunday Meetings. Here Snowball enthusiastically puts forward the numerous schemes he has devised for the improvement of the animals' life, health and welfare. The only one of these schemes that has any success is that which encourages them to learn to read. Again it is Snowball who, when it is discovered that many of the animals are too stupid to learn even the seven fundamental principles of Animalism, reduces the commandments to one simple rule – a slogan that they can mindlessly bleat out.

Snowball's greatest triumph is the clever strategy and personal bravery with which he brings about the defeat of Mr Jones and the forces of the 'counter-revolution' at the Battle of the Cowshed. There is no doubt about his exceptional contribution here. He is even awarded a medal. It is just this outstanding personal contribution that Napoleon will have to 'reinterpret' later when he has exiled Snowball from the farm and is building up his own personal prestige and dictatorship.

The principal disagreements between Napoleon and Snowball centre on two issues. The first of these is whether the ideals of Animalism should be so effectively spread to the surrounding farms that the other animals will rise up against their human oppressors and so become allies, or whether, as Napoleon thinks, the inhabitants of Animal Farm should prepare themselves for attack. This reflects the differences between the thinking of Trotsky and Stalin. Trotsky believed in the world-wide spread of communism, while Stalin believed that the Russians should secure their own communist empire.

The second and more important issue that divides the two pigs concerns Snowball's plans to build the windmill. In terms of the political allegory of *Animal Farm* the building of the windmill suggests the great importance Trotsky laid on modernizing Russian industry. Just like Trotsky, Snowball has high hopes for what industrialisation can achieve. Napoleon will apparently have none of this. He believes that the animals should first secure their agricultural production and so the means to live. Similarly Stalin believed that it was vital to gain effective control over Russian agriculture. He set out to 'collectivize' the farms. This meant taking them out of the hands of the peasants and placing them under state control. Napoleon pretends to have complete contempt for Snowball's plans for the windmill. This is shown most clearly when he urinates on Snowball's drawings and calculations.

Snowball's considerable powers of persuasion, however, convince many of the other animals of the benefits to be gained from the building of the windmill. Napoleon has realized that he will never be able successfully to oppose Snowball through the debates at the Sunday Meetings. Instead, when Snowball is fervently describing the benefits that technology will bring, he summons up his specially trained dogs and has Snowball chased from the farm. We see here how a dictator gains control through violence and intimidation. In a similar way Stalin eventually had Trotsky sent into exile.

Snowball is never seen again. None the less Napoleon uses him for his own purposes. Once Napoleon is in complete command, he begins the progressive destruction of his rival's reputation, minimizing his part in the Battle of the Cowshed and pretending that the plans for the windmill were his own all along.

Napoleon also uses alleged support of Snowball as a reason for executing many of the animals during the horrific series of purges he inflicts on the farm. In terms of the political allegory we can see Napoleon's use of his rival's reputation in similar terms to the use Stalin later made of memories of Trotsky. Every accident that happens on the farm (the first destruction of the windmill, for example) can be blamed on Snowball and his sympathizers. By instituting a reign of terror, in which any animal who seems to sympathize with Snowball is destroyed, Napoleon builds up his own personal power. Even when he is no longer visible, Snowball is still an influential force.

SQUEALER

Tyrannies are maintained by means of lies, by devious and subtle manipulations of the truth and by the twisting of words. This is called propaganda, and Squealer is the pigs' propaganda agent. Squealer's name suggests his true nature. We are told that he has twinkling eyes and a shrill voice. He is restless, agile and so brilliant a talker that he can persuade anyone that black is white.

Squealer is of tremendous use to the pigs, especially after the routing of Snowball. Every time Napoleon acts in a dictatorial way, Squealer manages to silence opposition. This he does partly through his devious speeches, partly through the fear aroused by the dogs who always surround him, and partly through the subtle but evil changes he makes to the Seven Commandments painted on the barn wall.

Squealer is presented throughout as a particularly corrupt and hypocritical animal, one whose sole interest lies in serving himself by serving his master. Truth and honesty are of no importance to a propaganda agent. They are of no importance to Squealer either.

BOXER

Boxer is the most tragic character in *Animal Farm*. He is Orwell's representative of the ordinary working man. It is for such figures as these that the revolution first took place. But of all the animals, Boxer is perhaps the one most cruelly betrayed.

Orwell presents Boxer as immensely strong, immensely hard-working and utterly loyal. It is the power of Boxer's muscles that is essential to every project, whether this be working in the fields or building and rebuilding the windmill. Boxer thus defines the place of ordinary working people in society.

We are told in the first chapter that Boxer is a gentle creature and also rather stupid. This makes us all the more angry when he is constantly betrayed by his masters. None the less, Orwell's portrait of Boxer – and hence of the ordinary working man – is not without its note of criticism. For example, the fact that Boxer's limited intelligence means that he never learns to read results in his almost entirely unquestioning support of the pigs. He never learns to think for himself. In addition he adopts two mottoes. One is 'Napoleon is always right'. This he adheres to absolutely, with the result that if he is sometimes puzzled by his leader's decisions, he almost never challenges them, nor permits himself the dignity of asking questions and demanding answers. On the one occasion that he does question a decision, he quickly accepts that if Napoleon says it, then it is undoubtedly true. In such ways he allows the pigs to tyrannize him. He is the victim of his own blind loyalty.

The second motto Boxer adopts is 'I will work harder'. In the end he works himself to death. Throughout the novel he is shown to work harder than any of the other animals. His cockerel wakes him earlier and earlier and he labours in his free time as well. As he gets older, Boxer dreams of finishing the windmill and then retiring. The pigs have promised lavish retirement benefits, but these never come about. Even the field set aside for retired animals is taken over by Napoleon for growing his barley – and we know that this barley goes to making his beer.

When Boxer finally collapses, the most tragic scene in the novel takes place. Napoleon and Squealer pretend that Boxer is to be taken off to a nearby animal hospital. In fact Boxer is sold to the knacker's yard. So much, we may say, for the good of the ordinary working animals under Animalism. When they are no longer of use they are not rewarded for a lifetime's efforts. Their bodies are sold for cash and – most horribly of all – that cash goes to buying whisky for the pigs.

CLOVER

If Boxer is the most tragic animal in the book, Clover is the most pathetic. Like Boxer she is strong, patient and utterly loyal. Like him she works hard. This is why she is so convincing when she accuses Mollie of siding with the human beings and allowing them to pamper her; her behaviour is not hypocritical.

Clover is, perhaps, slightly more intelligent than her husband. Certainly as Napoleon's tyranny becomes more established she is led to question some of his decisions. She even goes to consult the Seven Commandments painted on the barn wall. Each time she does this she finds that the commandments have been slyly altered. Instead of this raising doubts in her mind, however, she believes she must have remembered the commandments wrongly. Instead of asking questions she accepts the pigs' explanations of things and so allows the pigs to tyrannize her just as they do the other animals.

Two scenes in particular bring out the pathos of Clover. The first is when she sings 'Beasts of England' after the mass slaughters and is then told by Squealer that the song has been banned. The second is Orwell's portrayal of her desperation when Boxer is taken off to the knacker's yard. Her reactions here are deeply moving and help to convince us of the utterly despicable nature of the revolution. Finally it is Clover – old, going blind, but loyal to the last – who leads the animals up to the farmhouse at the close of work to watch the utter betrayal of all they have worked and suffered for, when Napoleon is seen playing cards with the human beings.

MOLLIE

Mollie is the frivolous little horse who is the first of the animals to betray the revolution by siding with the humans. In terms of the political allegory of *Animal Farm* she represents the White Russians, those groups among the Russian people who could not sympathize with the aims of the revolution.

Orwell shows us that this is not an intellectual or moral decision on Mollie's part. Though she learns to read just well enough to spell out her name, Mollie is no thinker. Her only interest is in her own comfort. When the animals invade the farmhouse, she is captivated by the luxuries that the humans have accumulated. In other words, she is deeply in sympathy with the capitalists. After the revolution has taken place, she proves to be work-shy. Finally Clover accuses her of siding with the humans, or capitalists. This proves, indeed, to be the case. Mollie finally leaves the farm to work for a man who can provide her with all the little luxuries she feels to be so necessary to her life.

BENJAMIN

In a novel about ideals and the ways in which they are betrayed, Benjamin the donkey represents the cynical voice of long experience which refuses to believe that life will ever get better. In many ways he is a figure like Orwell himself. He is deeply loyal to the cart-horses – in other words, to the ordinary working people – yet he refuses to do more for the revolution than is absolutely necessary, because he doesn't believe that it will do any good. He is fully aware of how it is corrupted from within. It is appropriate that it should be Benjamin who reads out to Clover the last and worst change to the Seven Commandments, which declares that while all animals are equal, some are 'more equal' than others.

MOSES

Like Mollie, Moses is one of Mr Jones's pets. In other words, he is on
the side of the humans, or the capitalists. Moses represents the Russian
Orthodox Church, and is constantly squawking about an ideal place
called Sugarcandy Mountain, to which all the animals will go after
death, which represents the idea of heaven. What Moses implies by
his 'preaching' is that it really does not matter how hard life is on
earth if there is a paradise to go to after death. Therefore, since a hard
life does not matter, there is no point in trying to change it.

When the animals' revolt is successful and Jones is fleeing, Moses
also flees along with Mrs Jones, but he later returns, and the pigs
tolerate his presence. In terms of the political allegory of the novel
this represents Stalin's ludicrous attempts to make a peace with the
Papacy in order that the Papacy would condone his actions in Poland.
This was an aspect of Stalin's foreign policy that earned him world-
wide contempt.

THE DOGS

When the dogs give birth to puppies, Napoleon takes them from their
mothers as soon as they have been weaned and educates them himself.
Right at the start of the novel it was shown that the dogs accompanied
the pigs to the front of the group surrounding old Major and, during
a lull in his speech, chased some rats to their holes. We thus see the
dogs as aggressive animals. It is for this reason that they make excellent
recruits for Napoleon's personal police force. In terms of the political
allegory of the novel they represent Stalin's awful secret police. They
are fearsome brutes and they constantly and loyally surround the
pigs. They are also the animals who commit the murders at Napoleon's
purges. The dogs, or secret police, are thus the raw power with which
tyranny supports itself.

THE HENS

In his speech at the start of the novel old Major declares that it is the hens' right to rear their chicks rather than have their eggs taken and sold. When Napoleon eventually decides that their eggs must be marketed to pay for the windmill, the hens revolt and smash their eggs. In this they represent the Russian peasants who preferred to destroy their produce rather than submit to Stalin's collectivization of their farms. For this the hens are horribly punished by the dogs and nine of them are killed.

THE SHEEP

Of all the animals on the farm the sheep are the most stupid. All they can do is bleat out the mindless slogan 'Four legs good, two legs bad'. This they do – probably under Napolean's orders – to drown Snowball's speeches when these are becoming too persuasive. So stupid are the sheep that they fail completely to understand the nature of the revolution and, when instructed, they eventually change their slogan to 'Four legs good, two legs better'. Partly through such stupidity is the revolution betrayed and Napoleon's power consolidated.

MR JONES

Mr Jones represents the force of corrupt capitalism. While perhaps no crueller than other farmers – he is certainly not as cruel as Frederick, for example – he none the less represents those forces which ensure that the animals' lives are short and hard. He exploits the animals. It is the basis of old Major's speech – and the animals' initial reason for their revolt – that such tyranny should be overthrown. The tragic irony of *Animal Farm* lies in the fact that Jones's tyranny is replaced by one just as bad, if not worse.

Jones is revealed to be a man whose energies have been sapped, in particular by the loss of money in a recent lawsuit. In the very first paragraph of the novel it is said that he has been drinking too much (a vice that will also be adopted by the pigs) and, as the novel progresses, Jones becomes more and more of a drunkard. By this Orwell is perhaps suggesting that the forces of capitalism are undermined by their own weakness. Eventually Jones gets too drunk even to feed his animals and they spontaneously revolt. In terms of the political allegory of the novel this represents the revolt of the Russian people against the Tsar when food supplies were short towards the close of the First World War. Jones is driven from his farm, just as the Tsar was driven from his throne.

Jones now spends most of his time at the Red Lion in Willingdon, where the other farmers are sympathetic towards him yet not really prepared to help, just as none of the European powers made a really concerted attempt to help the Tsar. Eventually Jones and the other farmers, representing the forces of the counter-revolution, mount an attack in an attempt to regain the farm, but they are driven back at the Battle of the Cowshed.

We are told that Jones eventually dies in a home for alcoholics.

FREDERICK

We are told that Frederick is a very cruel farmer who seems to take a delight in torturing his animals. In this we can see him as a figure representing Hitler, who treated Jews and other minority groups with a cruelty infamous in the history of the world. In his attempts to gain support from his neighbours Napoleon tries to negotiate with Frederick and eventually agrees to sell him a pile of timber. Frederick pays for this with forged £5 notes. In terms of the political allegory of the novel this represents the phoney non-aggression pact signed between Stalin and Hitler, soon after the completion of which Hitler invaded Russia. The German invasion of Russia caused extensive destruction, just as Frederick's invasion of the farm leads to the destruction of the windmill. Eventually the attack is repulsed, just as Hitler was repulsed at the Battle of Stalingrad.

PILKINGTON

Pilkington is an old-fashioned gentleman farmer who enjoys hunting on his dilapidated estates. In terms of the political allegory of *Animal Farm* he represents Britain and, more specifically, the conservative Winston Churchill. Napoleon tries to inveigle Pilkington into his negotiations with the outside world, but when Napoleon eventually sells the timber to Frederick, who then invades the farm, Pilkington refuses to help him.

None the less, at the close of the novel Napoleon and Pilkington are revealed as allies, just as Stalin became an ally of Churchill and the American president Roosevelt at the Tehran Conference during the Second World War. Orwell was convinced that they wanted to divide the world between them.

Pilkington is shown to be as keen to exploit ordinary working people as Napoleon is to exploit the animals. None the less, the disagreement that breaks out after their protestations of friendship suggests the period of mutual mistrust and hatred that existed between Russia and the Western powers after the Second World War.

MR WHYMPER

Whymper is the solicitor who conducts Napoleon's negotiations with the outside world. He sees that there is money to be made from doing this. His name sufficiently suggests his true nature. All the rest of the animals hate him. He is also the dupe of Napoleon's schemes, as the pig tricks him into thinking that Animal Farm is prosperous and that starvation does not threaten them. Whymper makes money out of his contact with the animals and he is presented as a thoroughly objectionable man.

Themes

Animal Farm is a short and powerful allegorical novel in which a group of farm creatures, taking over control from the humans, try to set up an ideal state, only to find that they have replaced one tyranny with a worse one. The events in the novel correspond closely to the events of the Russian Revolution, but Orwell's principal theme is the idea that all revolutions, though they may begin by promising heaven on earth, end up as a nightmare. All revolutions, he seems to suggest, are betrayed from within. This is a deeply pessimistic message.

The ideas of Karl Marx and the revolutionary activities of Lenin that underlay the original ideals of Russian communism were based on the belief that ordinary working people were exploited by the small minority of wealthy people who owned the capital with which they funded factories, bought and managed farms and were generally responsible for the manufacture of goods. While this small minority of people – the capitalists – grew richer, the people who laboured for them had no share in the wealth they produced, were worked too hard and were treated with the greatest injustice. Marx and Lenin believed that the time would come when these ordinary working people – the proletariat – would throw off the rule of the capitalists and, by establishing a fairer world, would enjoy the products of their own labour. In the passage from the Communist Manifesto quoted on p. 7 you can see how passionately such ideas were advocated.

In *Animal Farm* Major, the old white boar, has very similar ideas. These he sets out in his speech in the first chapter. Major sees that the animals are strong and many, while man is weak and few. The animals must prepare themselves for the time when the revolution will come and they can overthrow the rule of man.

Many of these ideas are attractive at first. Justice and equality make a deep appeal to the animals. And just as the revolution came about in Russia, so it comes about on Animal Farm.

But as we note that revolutions are built on ideals, we must also realize that they are led by individuals. In Russia the revolution was led by the Bolsheviks. In *Animal Farm* it is led by the pigs. And, Orwell shows, individuals can be corrupt. Once they have gained power, they are often tempted to exploit it for their own ends. It is a long-established rule of political life that 'Power tends to corrupt, and absolute power corrupts absolutely' (Lord Acton). In communist Russia, after the death of Lenin, absolute power gradually passed into the hands of Stalin, who became a dictator. In *Animal Farm* absolute power eventually passes into the hands of Orwell's figure representing Stalin – the pig Napoleon. By naming his character after the French emperor who started as a revolutionary but ended as a tyrant, Orwell seems to be suggesting that history shows how rebellions end up as tyrannies and how revolutions are betrayed by those who lead them.

The basis of tyranny is one individual's lust for power. In *Animal Farm* Orwell shows the means by which such power is achieved. By so doing he not only exposes Stalin and the Russian Revolution to devastating criticism, but also paints a general picture of the ways in which an autocrat comes to power and then maintains that power in the face of all opposition.

Orwell first establishes that the pigs are highly intelligent animals. It is a pig who initially teaches the ideas of communism to the animals, and it is the younger pigs who develop his teachings after his death. The pigs learn to read and to think for themselves. They also very rapidly learn how to exploit their fellow animals. There then emerges a divide between what the pigs say and what they actually do. For example, they *say* that all animals are equal, but what they actually *do* is make sure that any advantages that farm life can offer are theirs alone. We see this right at the beginning, when Napoleon arranges that any surplus milk should be given to the pigs rather than shared equally among all the animals. What Orwell is showing us here is how clever politicians, through a careful manipulation of events, can gather power and comfort to themselves by exploiting their fellows, even while they are pretending to serve them. Tyrannies, in other words, are based on lies, hypocrisy and self-interest.

This gives rise to another theme which was very close to Orwell's heart – the power of propaganda. We have seen that propaganda is the machinery by which politicians set out to convince ordinary people that the party is always right. This inevitably involves lies and distortions. Truth is corrupted, language is twisted and ordinary people are offered a false view of their world.

In *Animal Farm* Squealer is the pigs' propaganda agent. It is his task to justify his masters' deeds, right or wrong. Squealer is particularly suited to this task, since, as we are told from the start, he is so quick-witted that he can argue that black is white. He has a number of techniques for achieving this twisting of the truth. For example, he can invent spurious scientific arguments, such as when he says that the apples are essential to the health of the pigs or when he reads out reams of faked statistics to 'prove' that life on the farm is better than anyone thinks it is. In addition to this Squealer can employ his nimble wits to bamboozle the simple animals, as he does when he convinces them that Snowball's plans for the windmill were really Napoleon's all along. Furthermore, Squealer can build up the image of his leader until Napoleon appears as an almost god-like creature – remote, awesome and terrible. This is the reason behind all the parades and flag-waving that become so important to life on the farm when rations are running low.

Squealer has two further propaganda techniques. Both of these again show clearly how a tyrant keeps himself in power by using lies and cruelty.

The first of these techniques is to subtly manipulate the truth. The collapse of the animals' revolution is charted by the progressive corruption of each of the Seven Commandments of Animalism. After Snowball has been expelled, Napoleon breaks each of them. When the animals go to consult the Seven Commandments each time they think that one of them has been breached, they find that it does not read quite as they thought it did. What has happened is that Squealer has secretly changed it. For example, when it is believed that Napoleon is sleeping in a bed, some of the animals remember that it was commanded that no animal should ever sleep in a bed. However, when they read the relevant commandment, they find that it now says that no animal should sleep in a bed 'with sheets'. Old truths have been manipulated and new lies become the order of the day.

The other way in which Squealer persuades the animals to accept anything he says is by intimidation: he is always surrounded by Napoleon's terrifying dogs. We have seen that these are Orwell's equivalent for Stalin's secret police. The dogs are fierce, they growl and wear hideous brass-studded collars. Quite simply the animals are too afraid of them to dissent.

Napoleon himself is also adept at manipulating the truth to produce propaganda. For example, he is very careful to 'rewrite' the history of the Battle of the Cowshed so that his old rival, Snowball, no longer appears to be the hero that he indeed proved himself to be in the struggle. When Napoleon has used his personal police force to have Snowball expelled, we see the full force of his evil genius in action. Though Snowball has gone, every mishap that occurs on the farm is blamed on him. Snowball is held responsible for weeds growing in the corn. Napoleon declares that it is Snowball who is responsible for the first collapse of the windmill. The truth is becoming horribly distorted.

But far worse than this is the way in which Napoleon uses the image of Snowball that he creates to institute a reign of terror. To establish their personal power both Napoleon and Stalin needed to eliminate all criticism. This they did through a series of dreadful purges. Stalin sent millions to death and exile after 'proving' that they had been supporters of his old rival, Trotsky. In the same way Napoleon has many of the animals murdered for alleged complicity with Snowball. Scenes of dreadful execution take place. In these passages we see how a tyrant maintains his power. We see also how completely the old and high ideals of the revolution have been betrayed.

Orwell's criticism of Napoleon – and, by extension, of Stalin – is absolute and clear. He rouses our anger by showing the suffering that is inflicted on the animals and the deceptions that are practised on them. Napoleon's selling of Boxer to the knacker's yard is perhaps the cruellest instance of these. Yet the animals themselves are not wholly without blame. Put bluntly, they allow themselves to be fooled. This is partly because they are not very intelligent and partly because they are so blindly loyal that they very rarely criticize what is going on. For example, Boxer adopts as one of his mottoes the statement 'Napoleon is always right'. This is blind loyalty at its most blind. *We* know that Napoleon is nearly always wrong. However, by making it a point of principle to always believe his leader, Boxer makes it a simple matter for his leader to betray him utterly. This is a grim situation indeed.

Through the events of his narrative Orwell makes clear his absolute contempt for tyranny and the power of propaganda to deceive.

But he also has a further, complementary technique – his own prose style. This is so clear and so simple that it inspires complete trust in what he is saying. We are sure that language is here being used to tell the truth. Orwell calls his novel 'a fairy story' and a lucid, simple style is appropriate to such a work. Yet this is a very special type of fairy story. It has no happy ending, no kindly magic. If it is a fairy tale at all, it is a grim and bitter fairy tale and one that obliges its readers to look very carefully at their own political ideas and what they are doing to the world in which we all live.

Discussion Topics and Questions

DISCUSSION TOPICS

Your understanding and appreciation of the novel will be much increased if you discuss aspects of it with other people. Here are some topics you could consider.

1   How far is Farmer Jones responsible for his loss of the farm?
2   Describe the part played by Moses in *Animal Farm*.
3   What is Mollie's contribution to the novel and its themes?
4   Clover is a figure who arouses our pity. Decribe how Orwell achieves this effect.
5   Describe in detail the full nature of Boxer's tragedy.
6   What is Benjamin's attitude to the revolution?
7   In what way is Snowball an idealist? In what way is he not?
8   Squealer is a master of propaganda. Describe the parts that Squealer and propaganda have to play in the novel.
9   Describe Napoleon's activities up to and after the expulsion of Snowball.
10 By what methods does Napoleon consolidate his personal power? How does this relate to Stalin?
11 Describe Napoleon's attitude to the windmill.
12 Discuss Napoleon's negotiations with Pilkington and Frederick in terms of Stalin's foreign policy.
13 Relate Stalin's purges to Napoleon's activities in *Animal Farm*.
14 Describe in detail the last stages of the betrayal of the revolution.

THE GCSE EXAMINATION

If you are studying for the GCSE examination, you may find that the set texts have been selected by your teacher from a very wide list of suggestions in the examination syllabus. The questions in the examination paper will, therefore, be applicable to many different books. Here are some possible questions that you could answer by making use of *Animal Farm*:

1   Have you read a novel, poem or play in which animals or other beings represent humans? Describe how this is achieved and what it is designed to say.

2   Many plays and novels have a strong political theme. Discuss the politics of one such work.

3   Discuss a work of literature in which a knowledge of the contemporary history is essential.

4   Many works of literature are concerned with power. Describe one such work that shows how 'Power tends to corrupt, and absolute power corrupts absolutely'.

5   Discuss a novel or a play where ideals end up as nightmares.

6   Discuss the part played by fear in a play or novel you have read recently.

Glossary

apathy:	lazy indifference
bits:	the bit is the part of a bridle that fits in a horse's mouth
bon mot:	witty saying
bushel:	an eight-gallon measure
categorically:	absolutely, in the strongest terms
chaff-cutter:	machine to cut the straw left from harvested corn
clamps:	frames for containing harvested potatoes
'Clementine':	a popular American folk-song
coccidiosis:	a common disease in farmyard chickens
confinement:	time of giving birth
Crown Derby:	expensive and brightly coloured china
'La Cucuracha':	a popular tune with Latin American rhythms
deputation:	group of people putting forward a point of view on behalf of many others
dogcart:	a two-wheeled driving cart
ensconced:	safely or snugly placed
gill:	a quarter-pint liquid measure
governess-cart:	a light, two-wheeled cart
ignominious:	humiliating
impromptu:	spontaneous, unrehearsed
in common:	belonging to a whole group rather than individuals
incumbent:	something that must be done, a duty
indignation:	anger
inebriates:	drunkards
infanticide:	the murder of children
knacker:	a slaughterer of animals
knot-holes:	a natural hole in a wooden plank
licence:	moral looseness
linseed cake:	an essential part of a farm animal's diet
lithograph:	a print
malignant:	having evil intentions

maltreating:	being cruel to
mangel-slicer:	a machine for cutting mangel-wurzels (see below)
mangel-wurzels:	kind of beet used as cattle food
marshal:	set in order
muted:	excreted
parasitical:	living off another while contributing little
perpendicularity:	uprightness
piebald:	having irregular black and white patches
Politburo:	executive committee of Communist party
pop-holes:	exits in a chicken coop
porkers:	young pigs
poultices:	bread softened in hot water and wrapped in linen, for applying to injury
precincts:	outlying areas, edges
ratified:	confirmed an agreement
scullery:	back kitchen where dishes are washed
sentimentality:	soft-hearted feelings
silage:	green animal food preserved in a tall stack
skulking:	moving stealthily with evil intent
slag:	waste from a fire
smithies:	blacksmiths' workplaces
spinney:	wood
subsist:	to exist, keep oneself alive with difficulty
tushes:	tusks
vivacious:	lively
watered silk:	expensive, patterned silk